VOICES OF A
GENERATION

VOICES OF A
GENERATION

···

*Teenage Girls Report
About Their Lives Today*

···

Pamela Haag and the AAUW Educational Foundation

MARLOWE & COMPANY
NEW YORK

Published by
Marlowe & Company
841 Broadway, 4th Floor
New York, NY 10003

Voices of a Generation: Teenage Girls Report About Their Lives Today
Copyright © 2000 by American Association of University Women
Educational Foundation

Library of Congress Cataloging-in-Publication Data

Haag, Pamela.
    Voices of a generation : teenage girls report about their lives today /
by the American Association of University Women Educational Foundation.
        p. cm.
    Written by Pamela Haag.
    Originally published: Washington, D.C.: AAUW, ©1999.
    Includes bibliographical references and index.
    ISBN 1–56924-624-6
    1. Teenage girls—United States—Psychology. 2. Teenage girls—
United States—Sexual behavior. 3. Teenage girls—Education—United
States. 4. Peer pressure in adolescence—United States. 5. Self-esteem in
adolescence—United States. I. American Association of University
Women. Educational Foundation. II. Title.

HQ798.H28 2000
                                                      99–045385

Manufactured in the United States of America
Distributed by Publishers Group West

Contents

....

Acknowledgments

Heading the list of people who deserve a generous share of the credit for this report are those who conceived and implemented AAUW's innovative Sister-to-Sister Summit program, a nationwide series of forums on such issues as pregnancy, violence, and body image. Without the Sister-to-Sister program, this research would not exist.

AAUW's 1997–99 Program Development Committee played a key role, along with AAUW Educational Foundation Director Karen Sloan Lebovich and former AAUW Educational Foundation Research Director Priscilla Little, in helping to envision Sister-to-Sister. Special thanks to April Osajima, AAUW's associate director for program, and her staff for developing the project and providing extensive technical assistance. Thanks to Jodi Lipson and Lisa Cain in AAUW's Communications Department for their help in promoting the program.

The Sister-to-Sister Summits owe their success to the hard work of scores of dedicated adults and girls in community after community across the country. Sincere thanks to the AAUW branches and states, coalition partners, and funders that hosted Sister-to-Sister Summits in 1997–98. These branches and states are listed in Appendix B.

The summits that contributed data to this report, cited within the research, deserve special thanks. These summits performed an invaluable service by sharing their results with the Educational Foundation for use by the broader community of educators, researchers, and others who care about girls.

Once the 1997–98 summits ended and their data was compiled and analyzed, another phase of the work began.

Professor Michelle Fine of the City University of New York made an invaluable contribution in encouraging the research initially and in crafting the six questions that are the basis of this research report. Thanks also to her student Ronni Greenwood for her help in analyzing this data.

Several interns and girl advisers contributed to the honing of the questions, the processing and analysis of data, and to the editing and production of *Voices of a Generation*. Thanks especially to Cecelia Friedman and Sarah Morin for their help with the data and to Elisa Genoni-Zercoe for her help in synthesizing and analyzing the Sister-to-Sister "platforms for action." Thanks to Kelly Gilligan for checking endnote sources and standardizing citations.

Special thanks to our outside readers and advisers, whose keen insights and encouragement strengthened the report: Professor Barrie Thorne of the University of California—Berkeley, Professor Janie V. Ward of the Wellesley Center for Research on Women, and Professor Lee Ann Bell of the State University of New York—New Paltz.

For their contributions to the editing and production of *Voices of a Generation*, thanks to Susan Morse, Jackie Zakrewsky, Robert Brown Jr., and Johanna White.

Thanks, finally, to the girls who attended and planned Sister-to-Sister Summits, for your commitment, honesty, and keen insights. Through your participation and voice in this report, you have educated us all.

Pamela Haag

Barrington Area, Illinois, Girls Summit, May 16, 1998

Introduction

From a 15-year-old's summit questionnaire:

I'm sorry that this [application] is a little late.
I wanted to work on it a little more than just a
five-minute scribble so that AAUW could understand
what is affecting girls today and how.
I hope this helps a little bit.

Gilroy, California, #2, Asian American, 15

To the adult audience, the story that American girls in the late 1990s tell about adolescence is both nostalgically familiar—shaped around the enduring themes of popularity, boyfriends, and peer relations—and jarring in its hyper-accelerated exposure to sexuality and pregnancy, degree of peer hostility and sexual violence in school, and casual drug and alcohol use. In the family and in school, where many of these issues play out, adults may see them as uncomfortable distractions from the proper focus of academics. As a result, girls are left to struggle with adult-scale problems largely in silence and often on their own.

However, given a chance to discuss major issues in their lives, girls respond with alacrity. They are eager to talk about the pressures they face, which they describe vividly; they want the opportunity to share their opinions with their peers; they want to hear what other girls have to say.

In 1997 and 1998 the American Association of University Women's national Sister-to-Sister Summits gave many girls that opportunity. Conceived as a series of all-girl forums in cities and towns across the country, the summits focused on what has become known as the "evaded curriculum." The term, first used in the AAUW Educational

Foundation's 1992 report *How Schools Shortchange Girls,* refers to issues such as pregnancy, substance abuse, violence, and depression that can impede learning but that receive only cursory treatment in the formal school curriculum.

In developing the idea for the girls' summits, AAUW rejected several common assumptions: that adults know exactly what girls' "evaded" issues are; that issues are constant across races, ethnicities, and regions and even across town; and that adults, not girls, are best equipped to formulate solutions to these problems. The plan instead was to bring girls together in communities across the country to talk about the non-academic challenges they face in school and give them an opportunity to suggest solutions.

About the Summits

From November 1997 through July 1999, more than 150 Sister-to-Sister Summits took place in 38 states plus Washington, D.C., and Puerto Rico. The most effective were planned by girls or with the involvement of girls. They were sponsored by AAUW branches and cosponsored by school districts, colleges, and community groups and supported by local businesses, national retail chains, banks, hospitals, and others. Girl Scouts of the USA, Girls Incorporated, Big Brothers Big Sisters of America, and YWCA of the USA were national partners. Summits averaged 55 girls. The vast majority were ages 12 through 16 although some girls as young as 11 and as old as 17 participated.

The six survey questions that frame this report were printed on summit registration brochures distributed to teenage girls by teachers and community groups.

The questions were:

1. What do you think are the most important issues/struggles facing teenage girls today? [name three to five]
2. What do you wish you could change about your school, related to these issues?
3. What is something that someone has said to you that you wish they hadn't said? [give background and circumstances, if appropriate]
4. What is something that you know that you think other girls your age need to know?
5. What would you like to learn from other girls your age?
6. What is your definition of "sisterhood"?

Girls' answers helped local summit sponsors focus discussion topics; in addition, responses coded by age, race or ethnicity, and region were sent to the national office for tabulation. Summits typically began with a presentation to all participants and then split into several small "chat room" discussions of eight-to-10 girls each. The day-long conferences closed with the drafting of action ideas outlining proposed solutions to problems aired.

More than any other part, the chat rooms captured the essence of the summits. Each lasted about an hour, involved one or two adults as silent recorders only, and enabled girls to share common struggles and personal strategies for coping. Girls confided in one another, drew lessons from what they heard, and shared advice. Post-summit evaluations show changes in both girls' attitudes and actions following the event. Girls reported that summits changed "the way I act towards others" and "how I look at myself and others." Other girls reported, "I know now that I can speak about anything" and "I know that all girls go through the same things I do."

After the summits, many planners and girls pressed community leaders for change. They took girls' platforms for action to city council or school board members; hosted follow-up workshops on the issues raised; presented at conferences; spoke about the summits at area schools; and incorporated their findings into in-service training for teachers.

The Basis of the Report

Girls' individual written responses to the summit survey questions offer an unusually rich picture of respondents' concerns, conveyed in their own words and own voices. Self-identification by age, race or ethnicity, and region increased the value of this research tool. Full demographic data about the writers—age, race, location of summit—can be found in the notes for each paragraph containing quoted material.

The report is based on a close reading and analysis of the responses from roughly 2,100 girls nationwide who registered for a summit between November 1997 and December 1998 and whose application form questions were received by the AAUW Educational Foundation by December 1, 1998. Additionally, this report highlights more intensive analysis based on a smaller sample of summit application forms (730) that were systematically and extensively coded using qualitative analysis software. Percentages and numbers, when cited in this report, refer to the sample analyzed more intensively with qualitative software and to those girls answering the specific question being discussed.

Although numbers and percentages are useful to describe trends and frequencies of particular responses, *Voices of a Generation* is a *qualitative*, rather than a *statistical, quantitative* study. Because summit participants are self-selected—that is, they do not constitute a representative sample of girls overall—and because of variations in data collection, the numbers presented here cannot be taken as statistically valid nor can they be generalized to populations as a whole. Instead, they describe differences in the answers received and suggest trends. For a more detailed description of research parameters, see Appendix A.

Because the report captures girls' voices, it also preserves the way girls express themselves. Spelling has been corrected, but not girls' word choices. Grammatical errors have been remedied only where this could be done unobtrusively, without risk of changing girls' meanings or authentic means of expression. Italics are used in girls' quotes to indicate the author's emphasis, unless the text specifies otherwise. Where girls wrote words in all capital letters for emphasis, that capitalization has been retained.

Themes and Approaches

Education researchers interested in girls and school have often advised that too much research generalizes about girls without taking into account the often profound social, cultural, economic, and psychosocial differences that may exist *among* girls and *between* girls by race, ethnicity, and class. Taking into account the need for more analysis of "intragender" differences, this report is careful to note variations among girls where they seem interesting and meaningful; the portrait of girls that emerges is more reflective of a multicultural America and an America characterized by often stark class and regional differences.

The report does not assume that the white girl is a norm for behavior or values against which other girls are compared, but instead introduces multiple perspectives on girlhood. We approach racial and ethnic differences and identities not as essential biological categories with inherent meaning, but instead as cultural and social categories that shape girls' experiences of adolescence. Our intent in highlighting differences among girls, in other words, is to show the complex, inter-meshing social elements that contribute to the meaning or social experience of "girlhood." We see race and ethnicity as meaningful cultural constructs, but not as biological categories with essential or inherent relevance and effect.

We recognize, too, that class, linguistic, urban/non-urban, and national origin differences are often veiled under racial/ethnic differences and may be almost impossible to untangle in data of this kind. For example, some apparent differences between Hispanic and African American girls may in fact be differences between native-born or first-generation American girls. Class is a diffuse but extremely powerful dimension of difference as well and undoubtedly contributes to or accounts for some of the differences that are described here as differences of race, ethnicity, age, or region. Although this report looks for patterns of variation among girls, it cannot address all of the plausibly relevant sources of variation, so it concentrates on those differences codified in girls' self-identification on their responses—namely, race, ethnicity, age, and region. We present this data cognizant of its limitations and trust that follow-up studies will find ways to pinpoint further the social factors that contribute to some of the more intriguing differences that surface here.

Just as the report challenges a monolithic view of girls by identifying differences among girls, it also revises a common research and policy template that views female adolescence as a set of discrete problems, risks, and pathologies, ranging from drug use to teen pregnancy. The report is organized instead around the social relationships and "scripts"—or roles—that cumulatively shape girls' understanding of themselves. These roles include that of student, friend, daughter, peer, and sexual partner or subject.

Because the report focuses on those issues that adolescent girls see as struggles or problems in their lives, it presents only a partial portrait of girls' experiences. But it is not an abject or negative portrait. The report emphasizes not just teen girls' problems, but their resiliency—their ability to overcome what they see as obstacles. It examines some of the varying strategies, skills, and tactics that different groups of girls deploy to defuse tensions in their adolescent environment. Similarly, each chapter summarizes girls' recommendations to parents, other teens, the media, the school, educators, community leaders, and other adults on how this environment could be improved. Many of the messages and action ideas crafted by teen girls at the conclusion of their summits are synthesized and excerpted at the end of each chapter.

The variations among groups of girls by race and ethnicity, described in this report, underscore the need to have future data on education and adolescence that is disaggregated not only by sex, but by race, ethnicity, and class as well—and at the same time. Both quantitative and qualitative research supports the finding that differences *among* girls may be pronounced, even as differences *between* boys and girls overall have diminished in some academic and educational measures.

Gilroy, California, Girls Summit, October 24, 1998

CHAPTER 1

*"What Society Wants
Girls to Be"*

From a 14-year-old's summit questionnaire:

Question 1: What do you think are the most important issues/struggles facing teenage girls today?

I believe that today's teenage girls are often faced with the struggle or pressures of peers, fitting in, the way they look, comparing themselves to movie stars and models.

Question 2: What do you wish you could change about your school, related to these issues?

I would probably change the issue of grouping people and labeling them. Because of this, it's hard to make new friends because you're labeled as a stoner or a preppy.

Question 4: What is something that you know that you think other girls your age need to know?

I believe girls should know that we shouldn't have to change to fit what other people want.

Kalispell, Montana, #9, Native American, 14

It has become fashionable in recent years to view sexual roles and relations with a bemused "men-are-from-Mars, women-are-from-Venus" resignation that males and females differ in psychologically fixed and determined ways.[1] Girls' narratives from the summits tend to emphasize a different story—that of girlhood as an often bewildering social ideal that they sometimes aspire to achieve and at other times openly challenge. This chapter examines girls' varied responses to the icon of girlhood—the powerful cultural and media abstraction of female adolescence.

Among girls, overt discussions of the cultural ideals of female adolescence are not especially common. While many talk about the difficulty of meeting socially prescribed ideals, few directly assess the validity of those ideals. Asked to identify the most important issues or struggles facing them today, 104 teen girls describe concerns about "image and appearance" that are sometimes related to media ideals; 54 cite low self-esteem; 42 cite concerns about weight and staying thin; and 16 name the "media."

However, summit participants' analyses of girls' cultural prototypes are among the more detailed and expressive responses, particularly from older girls (age 16 and over).[2] Perhaps these respondents have already experienced the travails frequently cited by younger girls—concerns about "fitting in," feeling popular, and trying to conform to the ideals—and by age 17 have developed an intellectual and emotional foothold from which to scrutinize the ideals themselves.

Regardless of age, girls who comment on the social and cultural standards of female adolescence interpret them as problematic and in some ways unrealistic or distortive roles. A few girls write specifically of mourning a childhood that at age 14, in their minds, has already evaporated. "I would like to know if 'all' girls in high school want freedom but still want to be like the little girl they were," writes a 14-year-old from Salt Lake City. An older girl from Philadelphia echoes, "I'm only 16 years old but I feel like I've been around this world twice."[3]

> *... People are asking me*
> *"what are you?"*
> *I'm black and Puerto*
> *Rican with really good*
> *hair. I wish they would*
> *rephrase their question.*
>
> Cobb County, Georgia, #15, Hispanic/black, 15

Other girls explain that childhood has been replaced for them by a disorienting admixture of adulthood, sexual innocence, and sexual maturity that constitutes the social script of female adolescence. "I want to know how to live in an adult world, yet still be a child," writes a 13-year-old from Mississippi. You are "not a kid/not an adult," says another girl. A few other respondents urge adults and the media to resolve these ambiguities and "to stop putting kids in an adult role one minute and treating them like kids the next." An 18-year-old who identifies "girls and the media" as a major issue argues that "the media sells images that look like little girls in vulnerable situations. This still sets the stage for male dominance."[4]

Other girls characterize female adolescence as a set of inauthentic or ill-fitting roles that mask the "real" self or make it hard for a girl to "find the person she *really* is."[5] Girls are self-conscious about the disjunction between their own lives and the mythical girls' lives that society, in their judgment, creates and promotes. Girls, they say, face "pressure to be somebody they're not" and "struggle against conformity to what society expects girls to be." One respondent from Ann Arbor, Michigan, groups "what a society expects girls to be" along with "sex and drugs" as dangerous things she struggles against in her life.[6]

In a particularly vivid metaphor, two girls characterize the missing "true" self in female adolescence almost as a 1950s horror movie, reminiscent of *Invasion of the Body Snatchers*: "Girls struggle the most to fit in out of everything else in their lives," a 13-year-old writes. "We try to wear the right clothes, be slim, and not say the wrong thing. Most girls would do anything to get a boyfriend. Girls also don't stay *true to themselves.* While trying to fit in they become *clones of each other.* They need help finding themselves." A Carson City, Nevada, applicant indicts the clone-like artificiality in her school culture: "There are hundreds of kids that walk down the hall," she writes, "unable to dress how they wish and say what they *really* feel because of what other people think is 'normal.'" Tellingly, a 1998 study of suburban adolescence deploys a similar metaphor in asserting that

Girls' View of Prejudice

How large does prejudice loom in the lives of girls? Fifty-one girls call it a major issue or struggle: Twenty-eight say the problem is "sexism," 13 blame "racism," and 10 complain of "discrimination."

Complaints about sexism come from girls of all races and ethnicities, ages, and regions. They describe sexism in a variety of ways: One is wary of "under-education and gender barriers" related to learning. "Job discrimination" and "bias against women in careers" are the twin fears of two other girls. Another complains that girls are not "treated the same as boys in America."

Some girls feel, more specifically, that they are "put below boys" and that their major struggle is against "male

continued

Girls' View of Prejudice

continued

superiority." A Salt Lake City respondent blames "criticism of feminism," which she calls an issue in her own life. Although girls report "struggling against stereotypes made about women," one concludes that "sexism" persists. "It's a shame to say that this is still a problem in the 1990s," notes this 13-year-old from Illinois, "but it is."

"undereducation and gender barriers" [Central Brevard County, Florida, #34, black, 14]
"job discrimination" [St. Tammany Parish, Louisiana, #18, white 12]
"bias against women in careers" [Illinois #2, Hispanic, 12]
"treated the same as boys" [suburban Milwaukee, Wisconsin, #23, black, 16]
"put below boys" [Puget Sound, Washington, #23, black, 14]
"male superiority" [Kenosha, Wisconsin, #28, white, 16]
"criticism of feminism" [Salt Lake City, Utah, #16, Hispanic, 12]
"struggling against stereotypes made about women" [Minneapolis, Minnesota, #25, white, 15]
"It's a shame to say that this is still a problem" [Illinois, #88, white, 13]

parents tend to treat teenagers as "an undifferentiated mutant mob!"[7]

Girls' awareness that the ideal script of girlhood is remote from their actual lives or personalities provokes some of the respondents to characterize society and the media as pervasive but disembodied "outside forces" that impact their lives, but that they are powerless to shape. "I wish that I could change misconceptions about what girls can do and what girls 'have' to. ..." a South Dakotan writes. *"Society needs to change* from ideas that women have to be a certain way." A 17-year-old also offers this observation about society's role: Girls, she says, face "a struggle to truly find ourselves. .... *Society's working on it,* but there's always been an ideal role for men and women. What has seemed to be a role for women would definitely shape a young girl's actions, choices, and view of herself, especially since so many would feel that conforming to these roles would bring them the most love or the title of a good person." Although older girls have a stronger consciousness of social and political context than younger girls, and all are participating in community life (as evidenced by their attendance at a summit, if nothing else), most girls do not see themselves as agents within the society that, by their accounts, shapes gender roles.[8]

Other summit participants find the femininity ideal especially constraining because it seems to them so paradoxical and inconsistent. Some girls describe a tension between the vestiges of older gender conventions and contemporary realities. "While times are changing," an Illinois girl writes, "the prejudices harbored by society against independent women cause many girls to fall into an extension of the old stereotypes of girls as the weaker sex. ... Part of the aforementioned stereotyping is that of the girl/boy relationship as one where the isolated contribution of the girl is sex." One writer looks somewhat ruefully back at a time when girls "didn't have to always be so self-independent. I know women have fought for it, but sometimes I think it's gone too far ... Today's girls are faced with many problems. We are expected to be just as good as men because we've fought to be treated equally. We can't just be the damsel in distress. We have to actually be the knight in shining armor, [too]." Finally, an Auburn, California, applicant implores adults to resolve the contradictory messages she says she and her friends receive about femininity and give them "a clearer, more realistic definition of our general identity." Girls today "need a clear definition of girls or women," she says. "We are encouraged to be assertive through TV, magazines, and some adults, but we're punished indirectly by the world when we do."[9]

The vehicles that transmit society's image of girlhood, say summit respondents, are "teen magazines, like *Teen* or *YM*," "abusive pop music," "TV, which sends messages that glamorize violence and sex," "television and media body images" and, in general, "media depictions of teenagers." Girls who say they experience "pressure from the media" often explain that the bodies it displays are

[The most important issue facing teen girls today is] trying to find our identity in a male-oriented society.

Minneapolis, Minnesota, #43,
no age or racial identification provided

"too *perfect.*" A Kalispell participant laments "body images that tell girls to be *perfect;*" a Cobb County writer cites "perfection (TV images)" as an issue; and a Delaware participant explains, "We are also faced with always having to look beautiful....Even though guys don't notice how much work we do, if we didn't do it they might be a little disgusted. Also with computers, they can make models look even more perfect than they already are." Hence, when these girls "compare themselves to movie stars and models," they inevitably fall short of the standard set by the media.[10]

A handful of other girls, however, find fault with the media for flaunting bodies they regard not as "perfect" but as freakish. The bodies portrayed, they say, are unhealthy emaciated bodies that thwart girls' efforts to be healthy. One girl who cites media pressure as a major struggle uses the term "perfect" with evident sarcasm: "You can pick up *any* magazine and find the 'perfect' expectations of the 1990s women and men." Another distinguished "between healthy and fit, and a media-advocated thinness." And a West Virginia participant similarly implies a distinction between "staying healthy while society tells you to be skinny as

> *... Being yourself, in actuality it's fairly difficult. Media messages tell us to be a certain shape and size, our friends and peers want us to like certain things, our parents wish we'd act a specific way. With all the different messages from all different angles, it is sometimes hard for a girl just to find the person she really is.*
>
> Green Bay, Wisconsin, #72, white, 15

a supermodel." She casts skinniness as unhealthy rather than a specimen of perfection.[11]

In other examples, girls appropriate their own ideals of girlhood from available cultural reference points and imagine how female adolescence might find more satisfying ideals. Typically, these girls imagine a culture that allows multiple scripts for girlhood. As a Willimantic, Connecticut, participant says, "I wish people at my school were open to different interpretations of what a 'girl' has to be. Not everyone is skinny, shaven, and made up. I was called a snob for doing my own thing. I wasn't putting anyone down, I just choose to pursue different activities. Also, I am automatically a lesbian because I am masculine. I don't think I'm masculine, just strong."[12]

The ideal of strength and might—rather than skinniness, sexual allure, popularity, or beauty—reverberates through other responses as an alternative ideal for girlhood. "We women in general are the masters of all creatures (including man)," a 15-year-old boasts. "They need us, we don't need them." A Massachusetts girl, among others, envisions herself as a warrior: "We need to fight the battles we face and make it known that we will not sit back anymore." Similarly, an 18-year-old says she wants girls "to be remembered as fighters and not those who slipped quietly away, because we are worth more than that, and when we realize it, we then will be sisters."[13]

Conclusion

....

Adolescence in 20th-century America has been, at its core, a struggle for identity. Summit participants describe, however, the more specific nuances and contours of this familiar struggle in the late 1990s. Several girls write about their identity as a tense, sometimes skeptical negotiation between their "real" self and the abstract stylizations of girlhood that the media or, more generally, "society," promulgates. Some girls regard these stylizations as ideals against which they inevitably fall short, while others decry them as "fraudulent"-distorting or inauthentic scripts that encourage a clone-like homogeneity.

Still other girls respond to the internal contradictions in how adults think about adolescent girls—contradictions most visible around issues of sexuality—and lament the accelerated onset of adult problems and sensibilities in their lives. A few alternative ideals of girlhood emerge spontaneously in the summit responses—ideals that emphasize, for example, girls' physical and mental strength, or their status as "warriors" or "fighters" in their own service.

• Girls' Messages and Action Ideas •

Body Image and the Media

Messages to Adults

Toledo, Ohio: Recognize our challenges—females are second class citizens; we are stereotypes; the media uses us [to sell and consume].... Buy magazines featur[ing] POWERFUL large girls! Effect a media change!

Bucks County, Pennsylvania: Self-image—Let me find out who I am before you tell me. Be supportive of my decisions no matter what. Understand we are a different generation dealing with different issues.

Green Bay, Wisconsin: The expectations of media, parents and peers are powerful. Media is shaping our lives, and we don't like it.

Messages to Girls

Northern Westchester County, New York: Question standards set by Barbie and TV (breast implants and reductions; brand names).

Cleveland, Ohio: Have a summit with yourself every day.

The Schools

Salt Lake City, Utah: Peer discussions of consumerism—Commercials v. Reality.

St. Tammany Parish, Louisiana: Recovering anorectics and bulimics can speak to health classes or assemblies about damages to their health through their activities in trying to attain that "perfect body."

Allentown, Pennsylvania: Body image—the girls want the curriculum to include courses on self-esteem. They want counseling available for body image issues. They want people to be more sensitive to the hurt caused by negative remarks and actions directed at those that are different from the "ideal."

St. Tammany Parish, Louisiana: School uniforms create less stress on appearances and reduce cliques associated with clothing styles. In school, young women are judged by their appearances and are accepted into cliques based on their looks. They spend an inordinate amount of time trying to achieve the "ideal look."

The Media

Kalispell, Montana: Boycott TV and magazines that send negative body image messages.... Write to magazines and newspapers to explain the harm of negative body images.

Puget Sound, Washington: Media to show real bodies, not made-up thin ones.

Kalispell, Montana: Tell them you want to see models of normal sizes, shapes, and looks.

St. Tammany Parish, Louisiana: The media presents unrealistic, glamorized images of women's bodies that pressure young women to fit that description. IF they fail to meet the media image (fashion magazines, TV, music groups), they feel worthless and depressed and feel the need to starve and do other inhumane things to their bodies. The media should be encouraged to provide more realistic images.

Barrington area, Illinois: Media—show us "real" healthy girls.

Cobb County, Georgia: Girls—stop spending money on negative messages/images.

Tampa, Florida: Don't support companies that support racism.

Auburn, California: Form boycott and letter-writing campaigns to address unrealistic and/or exploitive portrayals of women and girls in media/advertising.

Washington, DC, Girls Summit, April 18, 1998

CHAPTER 2

"Sex Is Nothing to Play With"

From a 17-year-old's summit questionnaire:

Question 1: What do you think are the most important issues/struggles facing teenage girls today?

I think the five most important issues facing teenage girls today include ... the pressure of sex-related issues (reciprocal—pressures not to have sex as well as pressure to have sex) and discrimination (reciprocal—girls can be prejudiced themselves or they can be discriminated against).

Question 2: What do you wish you could change about your school, related to these issues?

I would like to see different approaches to sex—rather than critical pressures to or not to have sex, I would like to see girls educating and giving practical and objective advice to one another. As for drugs and alcohol, I would like to see the school inch away from the standard subjective approaches—I would like to see the school continue to educate but do it objectively—without pressure and order against the use of substances.

Illinois, #23, white, 17

S exual relations, interactions, and identity appear the most baffling and problem-fraught social areas for girls, judging by responses. Sexual violence, sexual risks—principally, pregnancy—and "sex" or relations to boys are cited 875 times by 723 respondents as "major struggles and issues for teenage girls."

Sexual issues crop up repeatedly in girls' responses to other questions as well. When asked what they would change about their schools, 10 percent of the respondents (66 total) wish that sexual harassment would stop or that male-female relations would improve in school. Asked to describe a hurtful comment or exchange, 144 girls (23 percent of Question 3 respondents) recall sexual insults specifically, delivered either by boys or girls. Invited to offer advice to other girls, 245 girls (37 percent of Question 4 respondents) choose sex and/or pregnancy as their subject. Polled on what they would like to learn from their peers, 94 girls (16 percent of Question 5 respondents) seek advice on how to handle sexual situations.

Summit responses show that girls perceive "normal" sexual relations, sexual risks, and sexual violence as existing on a continuum. This chapter will consider these categories individually, however, and note differences by race and ethnicity where appropriate.

Teen Pregnancy: One Reality, Multiple Perspectives

Girls cite pregnancy more than any other single answer as the "major issue or struggle" in their lives: 43 percent (311 total) of respondents name pregnancy, teen parenting, or "having babies." There are marked differences in response by race and ethnicity, with larger shares of the Hispanic and black samples citing pregnancy as a key concern. Sixty-two percent (109) of the Hispanic respondents and 57 percent (134) of the African American sample cite pregnancy, in comparison to 21 percent (41) of the white sample, 19 percent (11) of the Asian American respondents, and 31 percent (15) of the Native American respondents. Hispanics and African Americans contribute 35 percent and 43 percent, respectively, of the total mentions of pregnancy as the "major issue or struggle."

> *At this age, girls are beginning to like guys more than ever before. Many girls are being pressured to have sex from friends, peers, and guys. Even girls who don't get into these situations constantly hear about friends/peers doing things like that.*
>
> *Illinois, #88, white, 13*

Additionally, although the distribution of pregnancy answers by age mirrors the age distribution overall, an interaction between race, ethnicity, and age is evident in these responses. Generally, a higher percentage of the African American and Hispanic pregnancy answers come from younger girls—ages 11, 12, or 13. White and Asian American mentions, in contrast, are less frequent from girls at these ages, but more frequent at ages 14, 15, and 16.[1]

> *A lot of girls need to realize that it's not a race to date. Lots of girls feel pressured to date because their friends are, but their time will come.*
>
> Salt Lake City, Utah, #17, white, 13

The interaction of race, ethnicity, and the age at which subgroups of girls are concerned or thinking about pregnancy should be explored further, in view of its implications for when and how to target programs and policies to discourage teen pregnancy.

"Major issues" answers suggest another provocative interaction between the themes of "sex," "boys/relationships," and "pregnancy," by race and ethnicity. Only 24 percent (12 out of 51) of Hispanic girls who cite "boys" as a major issue for teen girls in Question 1 do not also mention "sex" or "pregnancy," more typically the latter. In contrast, 75 percent of white girls and 46 percent of African American girls who call boys a major issue do not mention sex or pregnancy. The numbers suggest a possibly stronger cultural, social, or rhetorical relationship for Hispanic girls between related issues—boys, sex, and pregnancy—that these girls frequently present as a sequence or trio of events.

Strikingly absent from girls' writings on sex, sexuality, and teen pregnancy, however, are explicit references to abortion and birth control, despite the controversies over these issues in adult contexts, particularly with regard to adolescent girls' sexuality. Only a handful of respondents mention these issues in response to any of the questions, although they may be intimating abortion or birth control when they describe "pregnancy" as an issue or struggle. Perhaps abortion has become a taboo subject or option for adolescent girls, perhaps it does not figure in their conceptualization of teen pregnancy, or perhaps it is so taken for granted that it is seen as uninteresting. In any case, it is noteworthy that the cornerstone of fractious 1990s reproductive politics in adult discourse does not appear more directly or explicitly in these responses.

"Having Babies Too Early"

[Western New York, #57, black, 15]

....

Subgroups of girls do not cite pregnancy as an issue with the same frequency—nor do they describe the phenomenon in the same way, ask for the same sorts of insights, or dispense the same advice to their peers on the topic. Recent scholarship on adolescence shows that the teen pregnancy rate and, indeed, the idea of teen pregnancy are not homogeneous across girls' communities and cultures in America, a point confirmed by summit respondents.[2]

In response to Question 4 ("What is something that you know that you think other girls your age need to know?"), 264 girls, or 39 percent of the question's sample, give advice about sex or pregnancy: More than one in two African American and Hispanic respondents offers advice about sex or pregnancy, in comparison to roughly one in five white and Asian American respondents.[3]

Rhetorically, girls' advice on pregnancy and teen sexuality also differs by race and ethnicity in many respects. African American girls, for example, are far more likely to advise other girls that "there are more important things than boys" in life and that, in a popular phrase, "sex and boys are not everything." Of girls using this phrase in their responses, 15 out of 16 are African American. A 13-year-old counsels, "You don't need boys in your life to get through life. Don't try to get pregnant just to keep a man near you because they won't always be there." Insists a Tampa respondent, "You don't need a boy to make you feel good."[4]

Advice to set other priorities instead of having sex to keep a "man" converges in some cases with the advice that men are "after only one thing" and are sexually "sneaky" and manipulative, if not predatory. Of the 26 answers of this ilk, 19 (73 percent) are from African Americans, four are from Hispanics, and three are from white girls. These responses forcefully admonish that "boys won't stay after pregnancy" and that "boys don't want females for nothing other than they are going to give." Another girl counsels, "Boys don't want love.... They only want one thing and that is sex." Gentle behavior can be a ruse as well, these girls caution: "The nicer the guy is it's just to get closer and closer every time." Another warns, "All guys are not nice. They may act that way, but not really mean it."[5]

African American respondents also are more prone to use a rhetoric that girls not "rush to be grown up" by having sex and babies too early. Of five girls framing their answers this way, four are African Americans. "You have

> *Don't let boys gang your head up, because all they want to do is get between your legs with that same old sweet talk line that they tell every other girl. And sometimes when boys give out their pager number, don't accept because they probably gave it to someone else, too.*
>
> Philadelphia, #18, black, 16

your whole life to get pregnant and get married," explains a Long Island respondent. "Wait until you finish high school and graduate from college. Then you'll be on your own to get married and get pregnant. But don't rush, you're only young once." A girl from Cobb County, Georgia, similarly advises, "Sex does not make you a woman."[6]

Concern about handling pregnancy and the demands of child rearing also shows up disproportionately in the responses of black and Hispanic girls. Some girls warn that "it is hard to have a child" or that "having a child is tough." Of the 11 respondents who give this admonishment, six are African American and four are Hispanic. "If you have a baby it cuts out all of your freedom," advises a 15-year-old from Illinois. These respondents share a suspicion that many girls minimize the difficulties involved in pregnancy and child rearing. Offers one, "Pregnancy and raising kids is not as easy as they think." Says another, "Teen pregnancy is no joke. I only know because my friend went through it. Her so-called man left her to take care of the baby herself."[7]

Asked what they would like to know from other girls, 79 respondents express interest in hearing other girls' opinions, rather than information or advice, about sex or pregnancy. What do other girls think about teen pregnancy, 18 of the 35 African Americans and 7 of the 23 Hispanics in this group ask. Only one white and two Asian American respondents want to know their peers' opinions on this subject.

The predominantly African American and Hispanic respondents who seek their peers' views on pregnancy and child rearing typically pose questions that sound respectfully curious. They want to know how girls made decisions about parenting and, more often, how it "feels to have a baby," "how it is to be

why do girls need to have a baby at a young age for love?

Minneapolis, Minnesota, #53, Hispanic,
no age given

taking care of a baby," "how it feels to be pregnant," and, in one respondent's words, "how it feels to have a baby in junior high school." One participant asks, "Is it hard being a teen mother?" Another queries, "How can they manage to go to school, and take care of a baby?" "I want to hear about girls who've had kids," says a 14-year-old respondent. Wonders a 12-year-old, "How is their life with a baby?"[8]

These questioners write about teen pregnancy not as an accident but as a "choice,"[9] though not one that they would endorse as optimal. Most are simultaneously critical of this choice, yet aware of and sympathetic to its origins. "Why," a 16-year-old wants to know about her peers, do some of them *have to have* sex or get pregnant?" "Why do most girls always *think that the teens is a good age* to get pregnant?" "Why do other girls that have babies think that that is *what they need out of life* at such an early age?" asks a Western New York summit participant. Others, who seem not yet to have formed a firm opinion on the matter, seek evidence that will persuade them one way or the other: A 13-year-old Hispanic girl who anticipates that she might want children in the not-too-distant future asks her peers for "anything, maybe something that would really make me not want to have kids, although I don't want to right now." [10]

Some respondents muse about girls' possible motives for "wanting" children: "Why do girls need to have a baby at a young age for love?" asks a Hispanic summit participant. Asks another Hispanic girl, "Why [do] some girls get pregnant just to have someone love them?" A 16-year-old African American concludes, "Some teenage females face neglect from families. They have no one to love them so they have a baby to love and receive love." These questions show girls' sensitivity to the complex emotional roots of pregnancy.[11]

Regardless of their understanding of these origins and motives, teens counsel their peers to delay pregnancy until they are older. African American and Hispanic girls are overrepresented among those counseling their peers not to get pregnant or, in common phrases, not to get pregnant "too early" or at an "early age." Of the 31 (8 percent) who advise other girls, "Don't get pregnant," 13 were African American and 12 were Hispanic; only two girls from each of the Native American, Asian American, and white groups offered this advice. Similarly, a higher percentage of African American and Hispanic girls recommend that their female peers wait to have sex or that they not feel rushed into sex before they are ready. Of 82 girls—or 12 percent of the Question 4 sample total—offering this counsel, 29 were African American, 29 were Hispanic, 11 were white, eight were Native American, and five were Asian American. One in four Native American respondents gave this advice, in comparison to roughly one in 10 white and Asian American respondents.

"How Dangerous Sex Can Be"

[Cobb County, Georgia, #1, Asian American, 13]

....

While many African American and Hispanic respondents describe pregnancy as an option of sorts about which they are curious, it is more common for the white and Asian American girls who discuss pregnancy to characterize it as a manifest "accident" about which they express less curiosity. In this, they mirror the prevalent adult assumption. The view of teen pregnancy as accidental in nature governs social treatment of the issue and conceptually defines most teen pregnancy prevention programs in schools. Because popular wisdom holds that teens get pregnant by "accident," programs in the 1990s emphasize sexual abstinence and/or focus on the mechanics of contraception.[12]

White and Asian American girls who dispense advice about sex and pregnancy cluster around two responses: They give information about these topics and, to a lesser extent, they urge girls to "wait to have sex."[13] White respondents, especially, tend to describe sex and pregnancy in terms of *prohibition, danger, risk, and threat.* Of the

> *If I stand up to a male jerk at school, he automatically calls me a bitch.*
>
> Illinois, #4, white, 16

27 white respondents who offer some kind of sexual information or advice in Question 4, all but five describe a risk factor (such as STDs or pregnancy), unspecified sexual "dangers," or sexual violence and harassment. Girls need to know, these respondents admonish, "how dangerous it is to have sex at our age. It's very scary 'cause you can catch something or get pregnant." Girls, they say, need to understand "the threats of sex," the "dangers in sex and drugs," that "sex is not a game," and "more about the dangers of having sexual relationships." Pregnancy, says a girl from York County, Pennsylvania, is indeed a serious mishap: "I've seen a friend of mine get pregnant at age 15," she confides, "and it ruins your life."[14]

For white respondents to Question 4, the threat of pregnancy or sexual disease is compounded by admonitions that they fight back against another danger—the threat of sexual violence or harassment from boys. At least eight of the white respondents to Question 4 discuss the problem. One recommends that girls know "what to do in an uncomfortable situation, for example, sexual harassment"; another shares her feeling that "when a boy keeps asking you to go out with them, then says he will even have sex with you, they are very threatening after a while." Others volunteer that girls should know "about rape and sex—how bad some people you 'trust' can be," "how much guys will take advantage of you when you are high or drunk," and that they "shouldn't go out with boys unless you know them for a long time." Consistent with their view of sex generally as a danger and a threat, white girls more frequently advise

AIDS and STDs

AIDS and sexually transmitted diseases receive very few mentions overall in girls' responses. Thirty-two girls—fewer than 2 percent of all respondents—name these as major concerns in answering Question 1 ("What do you think are the most important issues/struggles facing teenage girls today?"). Of these respondents, 12 name AIDS and 20 name STDs as major issues or struggles. These low numbers do not match the growing risk of HIV infection and sexually transmitted infections among teenagers especially: Nearly 25 percent of both new HIV infections and new cases of STDs in the United States occur in teenagers (those between age 13 and 20).

Urban and black respondents cite sexual diseases more than other groups do in answering Question 4 ("What is something that you know that you think other girls your age need to know?"). Those mentioning STDS here include 19 African Americans and five Hispanics, compared to three Asian Americans, three whites, and two Native Americans. Eleven of 32 respondents come from major urban areas. These respondents may see the effects of HIV, AIDS and STDs more often in their communities or lives.

their peers to learn "self-defense" and to know "how to defend yourself." (Of the 19 girls who give advice about sexual violence, 13 are white, three are African American, two are Asian, and one is Hispanic).[15]

Girls appear not to differ in their understanding that high-risk (unprotected or early) sex and early pregnancy are "major issues and struggles" for teen girls in general. However, girls perceive and describe these issues somewhat differently by race and ethnicity, and their vulnerability to these problems also seems to vary accordingly. Some girls view teen pregnancy as a "choice" from among limited options prompted by a need for love or a sense of purpose, an eagerness to be an adult, a desire for social status, or perhaps, as some researchers have found, a lack of incentive to defer parenthood and positive emotional incentives to become a parent in some relatively cohesive, low-income urban communities.[16]

Others describe pregnancy, echoing the emphasis of pregnancy prevention programs, as an "accident," a "danger," and a threat. In their responses, summit participants touch on related psychological, economic, cultural, educational, and social issues that many of them view as much the "cause" of teen pregnancy as the immediate "accident" that results in conception. Girls' wide range of responses here has implications for school policy: A "one size fits all" approach to teen pregnancy prevention in schools is not likely to meet all girls' needs because girls' views of pregnancy and sexual risks vary according to social and cultural contexts.[17]

Sexual harassment or remarks based on the fact that a girl is a girl, and sexual activity are ... important issues/struggles that face girls today.

[Kalispell, Montana #1, white, no age given]

"Sexual Disrespect Toward Women" in School

[Illinois, #4, white, 16]

Sexual coercion is a concern that crosses racial and ethnic lines. Seventeen percent (137 total) of Question 1 respondents explicitly identify some form of sexual coercion as a major issue for teen girls (although girls who named "sex" or "boys" may also have had violence in mind). Of these, 56 (8 percent of the Question 1 sample) specify "sexual harassment/teasing," 44 (6 percent) specify "rape/date rape," and 37 (5 percent) specify "pressure to have sex/getting pressured into sex" as major issues in their lives. There are fewer racial and ethnic variations among this set of answers than in the pregnancy and sexual risk answers. African American girls in the sample cite "rape" at a slightly greater frequency than other groups (9 percent, compared to 6 percent of the sample overall). White girls cite "pressure to have sex" more frequently (8 percent) than girls of any other ethnic or racial subgroup (between 4 and 5 percent).

By age, the only group *not* to mention "pressure to have sex" at all are the 11-year-olds. The answer appears with some regularity in all of the other age groups, suggesting that interventions against teen sexual violence need to be initiated early, a recommendation made in some of the girls' action proposals. Boys don't get all the blame for pressure to have sex; some girls clarify that the problem encompasses both unwanted advances from boys and persuasion from their female peers: "There is a lot of pressure on teenage girls to have sex," explains a 14-year-old. "This pressure not only comes from our boyfriends; it also comes from our [girl] friends."[18]

The "Culture of Sexual Harassment" in School

Sexual harassment comes up not only as a "major issue," but also in response to Question 2 ("What do you wish you could change about your school ...?"). Forty girls (6 percent of the Question 2 sample) mention the problem here. Of these, 27 girls simply want "no more harassment" in the schools; 13 girls wish that schools would develop and enforce policies to deter harassment. All told, sexual harassment receives 96 direct mentions from 78 girls (11 percent of the samples) in Questions 1 and 2 combined.[19]

The incidence of these mentions should not be misconstrued to suggest that girls alone are victims of sexual harassment. *Hostile Hallways: The AAUW Survey on Sexual Harassment in America's Schools* (1993) and subsequent research have found that both boys and girls report being targets of harassment. At the same time, both groups admit that they harass peers in school with alarming frequency. Fully four out of five 8th to 11th graders surveyed (81 percent) report that they have been the target of sexual harassment, with 85 percent of girls and 76 percent of boys saying that they have experienced harassment. Two-thirds (66 percent) of all boys and more than half (52 percent) of all girls admit they have sexually harassed someone. The fluidity of these roles—from target to harasser—prompts education researcher Valerie Lee and others to speak of a "culture of harassment" in schools that implicates—and affects—both males and females. Leslie Wolfe's research has found that many girls who perpetrate violence have also been its victims. Other research suggests that males who commit acts of violence are also victims of violence in other contexts; targets of harassment or violence in turn will harass others, and relational aggression is common between girls who are also likely the objects of harassment themselves.[20]

Someone said that I was a slut. You always try to pretend that what people say about you doesn't affect you, but it does. You slowly start to believe what's being said about you.

Carson City, Nevada, #25, no age or race given

A summit participant from Illinois recalls a case, for example, in which girls who reported an incident of peer harassment were taunted for doing so by their female classmates:

> In seventh grade, a group of boys made up a "flat chest club." They put a few of my friends and me in it. We told a teacher so they'd stop talking about it. All the other girls in my class were mad at us for getting the guys in trouble. One of them walked up to us and said, "You're so stupid."[21]

The effects of harassment may be more pronounced for girls than for boys; however, as Lee concludes, the ubiquity of harassment "suggests

It really bothers me when people say girls are whores or sluts. Most of the time the people who say it don't even know the true story, and if they did, it's none of their business. I used to get really upset about this in junior high. I was one of the girls with a serious (or so I thought) boyfriend. we didn't have sex ever, but people insisted on being concerned with my life. It sucked, because I wasn't doing anything wrong and even if I was having sex, it shouldn't matter anyhow.

Kenosha, Wisconsin, #37, white, 17

that the classic view of 'victim v. perpetrator' is an inaccurate metaphor for this social phenomenon."[22]

Notwithstanding the ambiguities of harassment as a legal concept, girls articulate their expectations from schools in straightforward, unambiguous terms: "Stop boys from hurting girls (by the things they say and do) and keep boys from touching you when you don't want them to," urges a 14-year-old from Toledo, Ohio. Girls reserve a crucial role for adults in punishing harassment: A Kansas City, Missouri, girl dreams, for example, of "a school where the adults in charge could punish anyone who makes fun or does anything to hurt anyone."[23]

However, a few girls who have reported incidents of harassment describe nonchalant or indifferent responses from school officials. A lackadaisical response to reports of harassment, as researcher Nan Stein makes clear, sends the dual message that the behavior is acceptable and that girls' efforts to change it are futile. Make "teachers and authorities [aware] that this isn't just one big joke and that this happens," recommends a California summit participant. Another similarly underscores, "Make teachers REACT when students do/say things which are damaging to girls." Finally, a Westchester County, New York, participant wishes schools would "pay more attention to the people who report sexual harassment."[24]

Other girls describe rules or policies against harassment almost as quixotic ideals, unaware that their school districts and educators might already have policies in place or legal responsibilities to redress harassment in school. "I wish there were less sexual disrespect toward women," writes an Illinois respondent. "I wish we had a specific rule against it." A 14-year-old hopes "that if a girl is sexually harassed there would be severe punishment to those who harass them." A North Carolina participant wants "stronger laws or laws about put-downs and personal questions."[25]

"People Always Call Me Names I Don't Like"

[Western New York, #34, Hispanic, 14]

A climate of harassment in school—not as extreme as physical violence but still damaging—is captured in girls' responses to Question 3 ("What is something that someone has said to you that you wish they hadn't said?"). These responses describe a gray region between what researcher Nan Stein calls sexual "teasing" and "bullying," a region characterized by sexual taunts, innuendo, rumors, insults, and aspersions such as "slut" or "bitch."[26] Twenty-three percent (144) of Question 3 respondents recall this sort of sexual aspersion as the thing they "wish someone hadn't said" to them. This 23 percent does not include an additional 25 percent

(152) of the Question 3 responses that describe being ridiculed for their weight, looks, body type, or personal style and appearance.[27] More Hispanic girls cite sexual insults than do members of other racial/ethnic groups. The 51 Hispanic respondents (32 percent) who recall a sexual rumor or insult compare with 24 percent of Asian American respondents, 22 percent of the African American sample, and 18 percent of the white sample. It is not entirely clear why Hispanic participants more frequently recall sexual rumors and slurs in these written responses. Perhaps they are targeted in this fashion more often than their peers in other groups, or perhaps they recall these comments as more vividly offensive because of personal, familial, social, or cultural values attached to sexual virtue and reputation.

> *Girls tear each other down all the time, slashing one another's reputation when they should be coming together.*
>
> Morristown, New Jersey, #1, Asian American, 16

Read cumulatively, girls' descriptions of unpleasant interactions (Question 3) form a numbing litany of incidents in which peers, primarily boys, call girls "bitches," "sluts," and "whores," and boys make crude requests for sex. "Can I feel on you?" a 12-year-old Georgia girl recalls being asked. Relates a 13-year-old from California, "Somebody told me they wanted to fuck me and get me pregnant." One girl doesn't find boys funny "when they say, 'Have you ever heard of Jenny? Call 1-800-JENNY.'" More occasionally, girls tell stories of chronic, verbal harassment: "'Do girls like to get their breasts sucked?' I really felt bad when he asked me this question because he said it over and over again. I didn't say nothing. This happens to me A LOT."[28]

Whereas boys may ridicule girls for being virgins, or because they "don't put out with guys," girls' put-downs may take the opposite form, labeling girls sluts or bitches for having had too many boyfriends or any sexual experiences; girls may invoke these slurs even as they also pressure peers to be involved with boys. Collectively, then, girls report being "policed" in two divergent directions by their peers. Boys push for sex, and punish those who resist: "My boyfriend pressured me into having sex with him," says a 17-year-old. "When I declined, he called me a tease. Now boys at school are disinterested in me because I don't feel I am ready for sex." Girls punish those who accede to boys' demands—or simply show interest in more than one boy: "This girl said that I am a slut for going with a boy I went with because I went out with his friend before him."[29]

Comments like this appear to be retaliatory tactics between girls, part of the sexual politics in school. One perceptive girl describes the way her friends use these tactics to enforce sexual norms:

> I was at a sleepover with some girls, and I stuck up for this girl they were talking about. Everyone started telling me I have no self-confidence because I was friends with a slut. It hurt me because the girl isn't a slut. She's just pretty, and she has to get punished for it.[30]

Ideals and Solutions: "Boys Would Respect All Girls, and Vice Versa"

[suburban Milwaukee, Wisconsin, #15, white, 12]

....

In addition to respondents who wish for a less sexually violent or dangerous school, 35 writers (6 percent of the Question 2 sample) make a distinct but related request that male-female relations generally would change in school. These answers—and similar recommendations in summit action proposals—do not specify that male-female relations be less violent, coercive, or harassing, but that they be less defined by sexuality and more supportive—both socially *and* academically.

> *I wish schools could change how guys view our young females. Males feel as though when a young lady needs something, he has it. The young lady starts to depend on the male and gives him anything he wants. The male treats the lady however he wants because he has what she needs.*
>
> Philadelphia, #17, black, 16

Significantly, this vision of a better school comes predominantly from African Americans, 25 of whom responded this way. In comparison, five Hispanic, four white, and one Native American prescribe better sexual politics in school. No Asian Americans offered this response.[31]

The plea for schools to improve relations between the sexes draws from an ideal of supportive, male-female *friendship* and camaraderie that is almost entirely absent in participants' stories of school life. As a Salt Lake City girl, just 11 years old, writes—in what is probably the only direct comment on this issue:

At my school, people can't be just friends unless they are both the same sex. Other relationships like boy-girl are not friends. They're further. I'd change that. … I wish that when I was friendly to a fourth-grade boy … the people I was with hadn't said that he had a crush on me. If they had not, I would have felt more comfortable around him."[32]

Participants who yearn for more harmonious sexual relations, of "males and females com[ing] together" or of schools "let[ting] us communicate more—to boys, especially," share a similar idea: that male-female relations are swamped with sexual innuendo and tension to the detriment of other collaborative relations between boys and girls as students or friends. "Men [should] stop thinking they can take over girls," says a Detroit summit participant. Another suggests that schools should try to improve "the way boys are during lessons." A third would like improvement in "how boys act about sex. And how they act about school." These respondents wish that boys' behavior was better and more respectful not only toward girls and sex, but toward education and learning as well.[33]

Sexual Identity:
"If I Don't Have a Boyfriend, What's the Point to Life?"

[Rapid City, South Dakota, #26, white, 15]

Fifty-two percent of respondents refer to "sex" (29 percent) and/or "boys" (23 percent) as major issues or struggles in their lives. No one racial or ethnic group provides this answer dramatically more often than another. These responses echo what education scholar Michelle Fine insightfully calls the "missing discourse of desire" in adolescent girls' sexual identity. Only a handful of respondents cite sentiments such as "love" or "sexuality" as major issues in their lives, and girls rarely elaborate on problems with "boys" or "sex" elsewhere in their responses in terms of their desires. Only a handful of answers to any of the questions describes a proactive female sexuality (for example, "*I wish that every girl who enjoys her sexuality was not considered slutty, and dirty. I wish that all the girls could walk around all schools with all the pride as guys have.*").

Positive references to lesbian desires are almost nonexistent in the intensely heterosocial culture that summit participants describe.[34]

Furthermore, girls' queries to other girls in Question 5 hint at a dissociation between sexual actions and sexual preferences, or even an inability to discern one's heterosexual or homosexual preferences. "How many girls actually WANT a boyfriend before high school?" questions a 13-year-old from Salt Lake City; another respondent "would like to know if other girls feel as though they can actually get to love a guy without having sex with them." A Detroit participant wonders if other girls "think having sex is fun." Two participants admit that they are puzzled, or at least curious, about "why … girls have sex."[35]

> *what do you think a real boyfriend/man is? 'cause I don't know.*
> Toledo, Ohio, #3, Hispanic, 15

Perhaps sexuality and girls' desires appear remote or disconnected in these responses because sexual expression seems telescoped onto actual physical intercourse: In other words, participants do not typically write of a domain short of intercourse where their sexuality could be expressed in less potentially dangerous ways. As a 14-year-old astutely remarks, schools should *"educate everyone that there are other ways of showing affection besides sex."* Sex, as described, appears defined heavily by risks—part of a jeremiad leading inexorably to pregnancy, sexually transmitted diseases, and emotional turmoil.[36] The accelerated progression described from having a boyfriend, having intercourse, and getting pregnant or infected with disease is evident in responses such as "kissing in middle school could lead to you being a mother in high school" and "sex leads to all types of diseases, and that's bad when you're a teenager."[37]

Since girls do not refer in these narratives to ways of expressing themselves sexually that do not involve the riskier behavior of actual intercourse, some respondents face uncertainty as to how they might behave sexually at all. "I am confused about what's too far with a boy," muses an Auburn, California, girl. "I *know not to have sex,* but other than that, if I really like him, and I do the things voluntarily, is it bad?" The middle ground of "not bad" intimacies or romantic companionship, practiced "voluntarily," seems to have vanished in these responses.[38]

The Double Bind of Sexuality: "How to Say No"/How to Say Yes

As scholars of adolescent sexuality confirm, "consent" and sexual desire are elusive concepts for girls. Lynn Phillips summarizes in her overview of adolescent girls that "recent research ... has found that many have internalized society's confounding of female sexual expression and negative repercussions. Consequently, many girls report feeling an internalized pressure to say 'no' when they actually do wish to express themselves sexually," just as they may also say "yes" because they fear repercussions if they refuse sex with boys.[39] Several summit respondents confirm this insight: They want to know, in their words, "*how* to say no" to sex.

"Just say no," explain some girls, is not enough to manage the social and physical consequences associated with refusing sex. Nor does the phrase acknowledge male pressure, violence, and coercion by which a girl's "no" is not respected or is linked to social repercus-

One time this boy asked me out and was like really not into any of my interests, so I said, "No way." Anyway, I wish he never asked me out.

Salt Lake City, Utah, #29, Hispanic, 12

sions. A Tampa girl writes, "I want to know how to turn down boys *nicely*." Echoes a girl from Auburn, California: "I want to know how to say no *without seeming like you're rude.*"[40]

These respondents offer a glimpse into the "rules" governing adolescent social contexts that make sexual pressure subtle and powerful: They fear losing their status as "nice" or polite people by saying "no" to sex. (In a curious twist, "women's worries about [appearing] nice to men" now recommend acquiescing to their sexual requests, whereas historically the "nice" girl was the one who resisted such advances!) These girls' anxiety about "how to say no" reveals a continuum from social pressure to sexual coercion to sexual violence. A Long Island respondent, for example, describes a progression from fear of losing a boyfriend to being "forced" into unwanted sex: "Some girls are being forced into sex by boys *and* because she is afraid to say 'NO,' because she doesn't want to lose him. She has sex and becomes pregnant and may end up with a sexually transmitted disease." A 12-year-old cautions that "boys ... can talk you into doing something you don't want to do."[41]

Alternately other girls wonder, in effect, how to say "yes"—or, put another way, how to say "no" when they actually may have a desire for some sexual intimacy. These participants want to know "how to resist evil *temptations*" such as sex and are unnerved by their lack of a language or safe context in which to express sexual feelings. As a 16-year-old Kansas City, Missouri, participant recalls, "I used to run away a lot. The first time I ran away, I lost my virginity. I was alone with a guy and he said, 'You want it. I know you do.' *I did, too. That was what bugged me.*" This respondent was disturbed that she might have wanted to have sex, but knew no way to, in effect, "say yes," so she gets "told" what she wants—and manipulated—by her partner.[42]

Adding to the double bind of girls' sexuality and the limits of the "just say no" dictum is some girls' belief that they bear personal responsibility for male sexual behavior. This sense of responsibility is implied in girls' conviction that sexual pressure, threats, censure, and harassment will diminish if *they* learn to say "no" more aggressively or courageously. A 12-year-old in Illinois states this idea bluntly: "Guys can get too strong sometimes and *you should be the ones to control them*. They can't think for themselves so we need to help them sometimes." While claiming a certain authority over boys by noting that they are morally feeble (albeit sexually dangerous)

A couple of kids and I were in the back of the school during a break and the subject of sex came up. This young man asked if I give up the skins. I told him no. Then he had the nerve to tell me to [leave]. I could not believe that he felt that way about girls.

Roswell-Alpharetta, Georgia, #11,
black, no age given

and cannot think for themselves, this writer, in a language evocative of nineteenth-century double standards, assumes the responsibility for controlling boys. Similarly, a Delaware participant writes that sexual pressure "is everywhere.... You have to be the one to push the guy off you."[43]

Summit participants prescribe a range of tactics for keeping male sexual aggressiveness in check. A California girl notes that "women always have to worry about *accidentally looking slutty* or like she's trying to turn someone on." Another participant maps out precise strategies for making "no" stick and for stopping male advances:

> I know that it is hard to say "no," but the way to do it is kind of manipulate them or tell them all of the things that can happen. Then most of the time they will say, "Never mind," or "I don't care." When they say, "I don't care," that is when you either walk away or start to yell.[44]

This respondent also has a backup plan, indicated in her response to another question: Girls, she writes, should know "how to use self-defense."

It is a profound irony of the "personal responsibility" discourse of the 1990s that girls should express responsibility for the incivilities or violent actions of their male peers against them. The pattern is consistent, however, with suggestions in these responses that some boys may, indeed, act as if sex is an entitlement from girls. Girls' hesitancy to say "no" because they will be judged "rude" or "not nice" reverberates in answers to Question 3 ("What is something that someone has said to you that you wish they hadn't said?"). Here, girls recall unpleasant exchanges ignited by boys' sense of entitlement to sex; 144 recall explicitly sexual insults and 11 report that they were insulted because they would not have sex.

"Once someone *told me* to have sex with them," a Hispanic 13-year-old recalls, "and when I didn't because I'm not that kind of girl … they called me a *bitch and a lesbian*." Another 13-year-old writes:

> I was dating this boy, and when he asked me to sleep with him, at first I said yes. Then when it was time, I changed my mind, and he called me a bitch! And never called me again and I really liked him.[45]

More specifically, boys may interpret a "no" to sex as antisocial or snobbish, as a Minneapolis girl discovered: "I get called stuck up a lot when boys try to talk to me. I tell them I have a boyfriend, and they call me 'stuck up.'" Acknowledging boys' sense of sexual entitlement, a Kansas City, Missouri, respondent advises other girls, "… Even if you're making out with your boyfriend and he asks—you don't *have* to do it."[46]

A treacherously paradoxical culture of adolescent sexuality, which seems to create a sense of pressure from peers to have sex—and, simultaneously, a sense of responsibility among girls for stopping males from getting sex—reverberates in girls' descriptions of interactions with boys. A 14-year-old respondent recalls:

> My friends saw this kid from school, and he walked up to all of us and said that we were really, really nice and that he wanted to go out with me. I couldn't at the time because I had a boyfriend, so it made me feel bad for saying "no."[47]

Accounts such as this, in which girls report feeling bad after they spoke honestly, suggest that girls feel guilty even for not reciprocating feelings such as "love." Relates a 14-year-old, "Some guy I just met told me he loves me and I didn't know him. So I didn't love him. I felt guilty."[48]

Not all girls are willing to assume responsibility for male actions. Some girls expect boys to take responsibility for learning how to act respectfully toward their female peers. Here, they write, schools could help: Schools need to "teach boys how to act," "give education for boys treating girls," and "teach boys not to pressure their girlfriends into sex." Ultimately, as a Philadelphia respondent writes, girls can get stronger and more assertive, but that is only half of the project: "Young men need to learn respect; girls need to learn self-defense."[49]

Adolescent girls face a mystifying array of sexual contradictions—in the media, by adults, and among their peers—that the "just say no" dictum glosses over. Summit responses underscore the insight by Michelle Fine and others that "desire" is a missing discourse in adolescent female sexuality. At the same time, responses suggest that "desire" is not particularly evident for teen boys either—unless we believe that violence, harassment, perfunctory sexual conquests, and hostility toward girls are natural expressions of male sexuality. Instead, boys' "sexual" expressions as they appear in these girls' narratives seem perfunctory and ritualistic, and appear to have little connection to sexuality per se. Undoubtedly, the survey questions invite stories of negative encounters more than positive ones. Still, in these accounts, sex appears as a weapon or tool to fix social status. It would require an especially violent and resigned perception of male sexuality to see these glimpses of teen boys' behavior as expressions of desire or of their sexual identity.

Conclusion

....

Through their individual responses and their summit action plans, girls describe complexities and paradoxes of adolescent sexuality and sexual activity that do not typically appear in pregnancy prevention programs. Out of these responses emerge several recommendations and cautionary notes.

First, girls' responses and action proposals call into question the timing of sexuality and pregnancy programs in the schools. Given that 11-year-olds are the only group of girls in the summit sample not to make reference to sexual violence and harassment, a conversation about violence and sexual standards in school may need to be initiated at pre-adolescent ages, a point bolstered by some of the summit platforms for action. Similarly, the summit responses indicate that the optimal timing of teen pregnancy prevention or sexuality classes may differ by race, ethnicity, or other social background variables. Hispanic and African American participants, for example, make more references overall to teen pregnancy at ages 11, 12, and 13; other racial and ethnic groups are more likely to mention pregnancy as a major struggle at ages 14, 15, or 16.

Girls express a basic but pressing need for well-communicated and well-enforced school policies against sexual harassment and violence in the schools, and several explicitly call for greater adult guidance and intervention in this area. For girls, a "safe, disciplined, and alcohol-and drug-free school" that is "free of violence"—Goal 7 of President Clinton's "Goals 2000" for education—would also describe a school free of sexual violence, harassment, and conflict in the halls.

Finally, girls describe vividly the "double bind" of adolescent sexuality—mixed messages about heterosexual activity and confused, ambivalent notions of girls' sexual roles and identities. The growing programmatic emphasis on "abstinence-only" approaches to teen sexuality—and the "just say no" axiom that supports it—may make sense in the abstract. Adolescents may indeed be too young, in many cases, for the complications and emotional complexities of sex. However, summit participants seek guidance on "*how* to say no" as they confront not only their own desires—evaded in many pregnancy prevention or sex education classes—but a spectrum of coercive to violent social, cultural, and peer pressures to be sexual and to engage in sexual activity. Some girls demand an emphasis on male responsibility for "abstinence" and civil behavior, and some state that they would like to learn how to express emotions and romantic feelings in ways that are less dangerous or less socially fraught than heterosexual intercourse.

> *Schools need to stop telling us that we should just be good and not think about what we believe good is. I think they try to get us to all act alike so that they can deal with us all in the same way. When we stop using our own judgment, these problems [sexual harassment, body image, sexual activity] start to come into play.*
>
> Kalispell, Montana, #21, white, 14

Other girls, in their action proposals, call for opportunities to develop camaraderie or nonsexual friendships and intimacies with boys through forthright, honest discussions of sexual relations at "brother to sister" summits or through coed social activities. Many of girls' descriptions and recommendations seem to seek adult recognition that girls are sexual subjects and that an array of social, cultural, and media pressures complicate the seemingly straightforward act of "just saying no." Some girls write of wanting to explore sexual feelings in an environment that is safe, less paradoxical in its views of adolescent sexuality, and far less focused on the act of intercourse itself.[50]

• Girls' Messages and Action Ideas •

Sexuality, Sexual Risks, Violence, and Relationships

Have a Sister-to-Brother Summit to Discuss These Issues Honestly

Suburban Milwaukee, Wisconsin: Sister-to-Brother Summit: to learn to communicate with the opposite sex.

York County, Pennsylvania: Boys need to be here, too. A summit, one with boys and girls separate, one together at the end.

Nassau/Suffolk Counties, New York: Begin similar groups in home schools and include boys. Call it "Sisters-to-Brothers". ... Have our school present programs on sexual harassment for boys and girls so we can learn together and be strong .... There should be programs about bullying in elementary school.

Savannah, Georgia: Need role models for boys—they need a "boys summit."

Educate the Harassers

Kenosha, Wisconsin: Educate the harasser. Offenders should be required to get help.

Lubbock, Texas: Dating Safety: Educate both males and females about appropriate behaviors and what is and is not abusive behavior.

Indianapolis, Indiana: Teach boys respect—have a brother-to-sister or brother-to-brother summit.

More Rules and Policies Against Harassment, or Rules That Are Strictly Enforced

Salt Lake City, Utah: Make sure the school has a policy [about harassment]; find out what the school policy is; make sure the policy is followed. Have orientation for staff and students.

Huntingdon County, Pennsylvania: Push for harsher laws against sexual harassment.

Fox Chapel, Pennsylvania: Girls thought that violence in schools should not be tolerated at any level. They felt that even mildly violent behavior should be severely punished. ... On all issues, girls felt that adults fail to recognize the seriousness of their problems, even when they approach adults with serious issues/complaints. Felt that adults want to bury their heads in the sand and to feel that everything is really okay for kids, even when it is not.

Morraine Valley, Illinois: Have principals, counselors, teachers aware and trained to deal with the reporting of any sexual harassment situations.

Cleveland, Ohio: No one deserves to be exploited by anyone or used as a sexual object to anyone. Make the word "no" a law that people have to abide by when you say so.

Have Safe Discussion Places or Hotlines in School—Organized by Peers—Concerning Sex and Pregnancy

York County, Pennsylvania: Have a hotline (peer operators) on teen pregnancy.

Huntingdon County, Pennsylvania: Have a hotline for teens by teens.

North Carolina: Teen pregnancy/sexuality—more hotlines. Open communication with your harassers. Learn from mistakes of others regarding pregnancy, loss of childhood and other relationships.

Carson City, Nevada: Have a way of asking questions anonymously and getting answers.

Detroit, Michigan: Provide safe/confidential place in school for girls to get together on a regular basis to discuss sexuality issues.

Make Sex Education More Realistic, "Graphic," and Honest

Huntingdon County, Pennsylvania: People teaching sex education should be more graphic, objective, and serious.

Jefferson County, Wisconsin: Gynecologist visits.

Willimantic, Connecticut: We want to have more information about real world experiences, for example, sexuality education, how to make decisions, how to initiate open communication, how to fight stereotypes, double standards....

Illinois: Use realistic language and situations in sex education.

Demonstrate the Effects of Teen Parenting and Pregnancy in Graphic and Realistic Terms: Have Mandatory Parenting Classes
Delaware: message to girls: spend a day with a teen mother.... Invite teen mothers to visit girls in a normal setting such as school....

Carson City, Nevada: There should be mandatory parenting classes.

Montgomery County, Maryland: Life skills–oriented classes—for example, carry a sack of flour as a baby.

Tampa, Florida: Make sure that all ninth-graders go through a course that demonstrates the responsibilities of having a baby.

Initiate Classes and Programs on Sex, Pregnancy, and Harassment at Earlier Grade Levels
Green Bay, Wisconsin: We want to receive more education earlier so that each of us can make a good personal choice about when to have sex.

Salt Lake City, Utah: Have a class on respect in all schools every year for third grade and up.

Barrington area, Illinois: Start education on controlling sexual harassment at a younger age (fourth grade).

Notable Program

Expand the "Baby, Think it Over" Program for Pregnancy Prevention

St. Tammany Parish, Louisiana: Teen moms to explain the changes to their lives. These could be readily available from the parenting center in Covington—actual teen moms still in school…. "Baby—let's wait." Should this be revived?

Carson City, Nevada: Expand "Baby, think it over" program to all freshmen and extend it to a weekend or longer.

Other Action Plans

Salt Lake City, Utah: Establish a user-friendly "help center" in all schools to provide girls support, information, referral, or community resources on the issues of sexual harassment, early sexual activity/teen pregnancy, substance abuse, and violence. If a "help center" already exists, the goal is to make it more user-friendly (accessible) to girls. The help center needs to have the power to initiate action toward resolution of the problems/concerns.

North Carolina: Have discussion groups with parents. Require them to attend with their boy/girl.

Kalispell, Montana: Presentation to school board.

Messages to Adults

Sex, Pregnancy, Sexual Pressure, and Decisions About Sex: Advise Us and Let Us Make Decisions

Allentown, Pennsylvania: Message to adults: The girls want their decision to be their own—not their parents' or their mates'.

Asheville, North Carolina: Teen pregnancy/sexuality—messages to adults: Parents should discuss with girls, keep us informed. Parents should instill good values but don't push your values on us. Teach us how to think and then respect the choices we made.

Kalispell, Montana: Advise us, but allow teens to make their own decisions. Don't criticize—it [sex] will happen sooner or later.

Ann Arbor, Michigan: We ARE growing up.... Take teens' opinions seriously—they're valid too.

Messages to Girls

Sex, Pregnancy, Sexual Pressure, and Decisions About Sex

Allentown, Pennsylvania: Message to mates: The girls want to learn how to communicate openly in an intimate relationship about sex and their emotional needs. They want their mates to learn that the relationship is more than just sex. They don't want their mates to use lies or other manipulative means to pressure them into sex.

Anderson, Indiana: We are aware that verbal abuse can be just as bad, or even worse than physical abuse. If we are victims of either, we will tell a trusted person as soon as possible. If we are in danger, we will do all we can to find a safe place.

Aurora, Illinois: Express love in other ways.

Cobb County, Georgia: Harassment—communicate clearly what you don't like.

Photo by Bob Ellis/*Cortland Standard*, Cortland, New York, Girls Summit, November 14, 1998

CHAPTER 3
"Fitting In"

From a 15-year-old's summit questionnaire:

Question 1: What do you think are the most important issues/struggles facing teenage girls today?

... The need to belong. Many girls feel that they don't belong anywhere or with anyone, so they begin to act insensibly and thus run into trouble. Many girls will do anything so they can be "cool" and belong to a group. For example, some may try drugs so their "friends" will like them....

Question 2: What do you wish you could change about your school, related to these issues?

I wish in school the teachers would give the students more opportunities to work with and cooperate with other students; that would increase the probability of making new friends for people who are shy and have difficulty in that area....

Orange County, California, #10, Asian American, 15

Summit data dramatically echo a controversial 1998 claim that, overall, adolescents are more preoccupied with peer relations and experiences than with relations with their parents and families.[1] In the sample overall, relationships with peers and friends appear with much greater frequency as the focus of teen concern than do parental relationships.

Girls refer to families and family problems in response to three of the questions. Out of 723 girls answering Question 1 (What do you think are the most important issues/struggles facing teenage girls today?), 95 (or 13 percent) list their "family" or "parents" as a concern. Few elaborate, but those who do complain of a "lack of guidance from elders," "tons of pressure on girls to get A's," and "not feeling loved enough." A small number of girls—15 (2 percent)—refer to domestic violence or "abuse," either within their own family or in families generally.[2]

References to family appear in response to other survey questions. In response to Question 3 (What is something that someone has said to you that you wish they hadn't said?), a cluster of girls (24 out of 617, or 4 percent) recall that a parent said something insulting or demeaning to them—sometimes belittling their intelligence or ability. In response to Question 4 (What is something that you know that you think other girls your age need to know?), a smaller number of girls (13 out of 671, or 2 percent) urges girls to "value" or listen to their parents more. "I would like girls to know that they should always try to get along with their parents, however hard that might be," advises a white 13-year-old; a 13-year-old Hispanic respondent insists "that your mom is your best friend, and never neglect her."[3]

Generally, however, parental relationships don't preoccupy summit participants as a prominent "struggle" or "issue." Their relative absence could mean that many of the girls enjoy nurturing or supportive relationships with their parent(s) or caregivers—so much so that these relationships recede from view as sources of tension or conflict. Or the absence could mean that most of the girls simply do not experience the parental relationship to be as interesting, significant, or troubling as other relationships in their lives. In comparison to the overall sample and to other ages, a higher percentage of 13- and 14-year-olds mentions family problems in the "major issues" question (22 percent and 17 percent respectively), yet age variations are not dramatic.

> *I wish the schools wouldn't have to be so challenging in the social world. I mean the "group," "cliquish," "popular/not popular"—these kinds of things.*
>
> Arizona, #22, white, 15

Variations in mentions of family issues occur, however, by race and ethnicity. A markedly higher percentage of Asian American (23 percent) and Hispanic (20 percent) respondents mentions family and parental issues than girls from other groups; only 11 percent of the African American sample, 8 percent of the white sample, and 8 percent of the Native American respondents mention these issues. For the Asian American and Hispanic girls, family may have a greater presence in their

Take a Long-Term Perspective

A comparatively high percentage of Asian American respondents advocate taking the long view in response to Question 4 (What is something that you know that you think other girls your age need to know?). Twelve percent of Asian American girls gave such an answer compared to 4 percent of the overall sample. Among the responses were these:

Twenty years from now it won't matter what you have looked like or who you went out with—but who you are.

St. Tammany, Louisiana, #3, white, 13

They need to know that high school is not your whole life and it certainly isn't the end of the world. There is a lot more to life than just the immediate time/place in front of us (although sometimes it doesn't seem that way). There is much more out there than this tiny protected town we live in and there are many more important things than popularity and high school concerns. Things that seem so important right now, really in the long run are not.

Morristown, New Jersey, #1, Asian, 16

lives symbolically, materially, or psychologically—an insight that would be lost under the general conclusion that girls do not often mention their relation to their families.[4] Given that the Asian American and Hispanic groups would have a larger number of immigrant girls, it is likely that family emerges more vividly as an "issue or struggle" for these groups because families undergoing a migration and resettlement typically do function more as collective units and exert more influence and pressure over their children than geographically settled families.[5]

Peer Pressure:
"A Big Pull Between Being ... Yourself and Fitting In"

[Green Bay, Wisconsin, girls' platform for action]

....

Peer relations are clearly a more dominant concern for summit participants. Fully 41 percent of the Question 1 sample name peer relations—
"peer pressure" (196 girls total), "friends" (69 total), or "popularity and
pressure to fit in" (72 total)—as a major issue or struggle facing them.[6]
Sounding a familiar adolescent refrain, a 12-year-old respondent from
Arizona says girls worry "if they are popular or not, if they are pretty or
not, if they have good friends or not, if they dress cool or not."[7]

While the peer relations theme is fairly ubiquitous, certain aspects of
it—"peer pressure" and the "pressure to fit in"—appear with greater frequency in some racial and ethnic groups than in others. White girls, in
particular, identify peer pressure as a major issue in their lives. Fifty-six
percent—more than one in two—white girls and 40 percent of the Asian
American participants mention peer pressure and/or the pressure to fit in
as a "major issue"; in contrast, 26 percent—one in four—Hispanic respondents name peer pressure a major concern.[8] Similar racial and ethnic patterns appear in the "advice" question (Question 4: "What is something that
you know that you think other girls your age need to know?"): 10 percent
of the sample overall feel that other girls should know how to handle peer
pressure better, but higher percentages of white (15 percent) and Asian
American respondents (14 percent) give this answer, compared to African
Americans and Hispanics (7 percent each). In Question 5 ("What would
you like to learn from other girls your age?"), white respondents comprise
41 percent (15) of those who would "like to know" from other girls "how
to handle peer pressure" better.[9]

Likewise, almost one in five (20 percent) of the white sample and one in four of the Asian American respondents highlight concerns about "image" and "appearance"—which could encompass worries about weight, style, clothing, and so on. Fewer than one in 10 (9 percent) of the African American sample and slightly more than one in 10 of the Hispanic and Native American respondents list concerns about their social "image." Of the 20 respondents who worry *both* about their image and "fitting in," 13 are white, and four Asian American. These numbers capture in shorthand some intriguing differences in how girls deal with the cliché of adolescent "peer pressure."

Girls who worry about fitting in and identify peer pressure as a major struggle describe social cliques and hierarchies in an almost bureaucratic language: There is "pressure to act in a certain way, dress a certain way, and look a certain way. When girls don't meet these '*qualifications*,' they get teased or ridiculed." As a Native American participant from Green Bay, Wisconsin, similarly explains, "What I mean by 'clique' is [people] only hang with one group of people who are in the same *classification*. I think people should float around and see everyone."[10]

In practice, not a great deal of "floating around" seems to occur for girls in school; summit respondents describe an awareness among girls as to how they rank socially, and a policing of the boundaries between groups through rumors and gossip:

> Self-image and how other people see you are really important to teenage girls. Although these things shouldn't be on the top of the list, it is sad to say they are. This includes clothes, weight, and how you look. Cliques are also a major problem in teenage girls' lives. You definitely know if you are in the in-crowd. Many of the popular students tease, harass, or completely ignore students not in their clique.[11]

Immersion in "the crowd," according to some responses, is in fact the primary goal of adolescent social interactions. "To be a part of the crowd or to be popular is a teenager's main goal," says a black Long Island girl. "So to fit in they will go to the extreme to be considered popular and cool. Even if they are going against what they believe in." The quest to be part of the crowd not only leads some girls to "go against" their beliefs but also seems unrelated to pleasure for some girls: "You are too busy trying to impress," writes a Kansas City, Missouri, respondent, "to have fun in life." Trying to be popular, explains another participant, may involve "pressure to have a boyfriend even if there is nobody you like."[12]

> *I would want everybody to mix, so there wouldn't be clans, like popular class and low class.*
>
> Rapid City, South Dakota, #11, white, 14

The tacit human "classifications" and qualifications that dictate where girls fit socially provoke some respondents to describe cliques and the "crowd" as antithetical to a *real* self that is unknown, and to some extent unknowable, within the surface-oriented world of peer groups. The major struggle, one girl describes in characteristic language, is "being your *own* person *while* still being accepted"—a phrasing that places being "your own person" in opposition to social acceptance. Another girl records her major struggle as "deciding when you're going to follow the crowd and when you're going to make your own decisions." A 17-year-old eloquently describes the secret, unknown self: "I would like to know which parts of [girls'] personalities have been *hidden* because of the things they have had to do to be considered accepted. I'd like to get to know the human being, and not the girl, *underneath*." Another writer poetically expounds that a "sister" "can look through all of the acts and walls you've built up to protect yourself from being hurt by others. Once they've seen through this they encourage the real you to step out of the shadows and let everyone see who you really are."[13]

Missing in the pitting of "the crowd" against the "hidden" secret self is a sense that peers might possess the ability to help a girl realize her authentic, "individual" beliefs or goals. In their descriptions of peer pressure, some girls—especially white respondents—perceive a grim choice between being

A big concern is, "Am I alone?" And the answer is always "no." I wish you would really stress that.

Green Bay, Wisconsin, #20, white, 13

alone and authentic or being part of the "crowd" and thereby inauthentic. As one girl puts it, "Sometimes your friends can be idiots and force you to be something you're not."[14]

The antidote, for many girls, is to "stand on their own." Thirteen percent (88 total) of girls overall advise their peers to be more "independent" of others' opinions, "just be themselves," or care more about "what's on the inside" than appearances. One in four Asian American and white respondents dispenses such advice, in contrast to one in 10 Hispanic and Native American girls and one in 20 African Americans. As a white 14-year-old counsels her peers, "It's easier to be yourself and not wear a mask than to pretend to be like everyone else. Be different." Offers another girl, "If you act *like yourself,* it will benefit you in the long run." Another participant "would like to know from other girls how they feel about drugs, peer pressure, alcohol abuse, sex and harassment. Not *just how their friends* feel, but THEIR honest opinion."[15]

Less frequently, girls propose optimistically to reconcile "fitting in" with authenticity. A white, 14-year-old summit participant shares her wisdom that "being a good person and a good student will get you farther in life (not only in school, but with friends too) than being 'cool' and messing up in drugs and other things. [Girls] need to know they can be themselves and still be 'cool.'" Similarly, an Illinois writer advises her peers, "Don't worry about what other people think of you and you'll be more relaxed, more like the *real you*. You may even find that you become popular being YOU!"[16]

Just as girls may envision a secret self "hidden" beneath the personae of social cliques, they recommend, by the same logic, that other girls "ignore insults" and hurtful comments from peers to protect this self from harm. They propose insulating the inner self by practicing a kind of strategic withdrawal. "[Don't] let other people's opinions get to you," admonishes a 13-year-old from Indianapolis. "I've learned if you sit and listen, then ignore, they don't hurt you anymore." A like thinker from Gilroy, California, counsels, "When someone tries to cause a fight, shut your mouth and leave." In Westchester County, New York, another summit participant advises, "You should remain calm when something bad is going on."[17]

Some advocate social dissemblance—appearing not to care about events. "When something is happening, don't *act* like it bothers you," advises one respondent. Recommends another, "There is nothing like lying down and *pretending* to be dead." A Long Island girl somewhat paradoxically recommends that girls act together to ignore boys' comments, which she hopes will signal to boys how damaging their behavior is: "I wish that we could have all the girls get together in a big room and just say, 'Ignore anything that is said to you negatively.' And then maybe the boys will see that making fun of girls isn't working." Another Nassau/Suffolk Counties respondent imagines a boundary between harassing comments that girls should "not pay attention" to and physical assaults: "Other girls should know that whatever boys say to you that hurt you, you don't have to pay attention. Just ignore them and if they attack sexually, tell a grownup."[18]

But denial and social withdrawal aren't viewed universally as ideal responses to peer troubles. A few respondents endorse counter-attack, either verbal or physical: "Ignoring the insults or sexism isn't always the best thing," insists a 12-year-old. "You should fight back, but not physically." Twenty-three respondents write that they know or want to know how to "fight back" and defend themselves, verbally and physically. The relatively few girls who describe direct confrontations over verbal insults—

I wish more people would have compassion for classmates and less people ridiculing each other and I also wish people wouldn't be afraid to reach out and help each other.

Missouri, #52, white, 14

usually over race and ethnicity rather than sex—almost uniformly boast of positive results. For example, a 16-year-old who comes from the Middle East says,

At one point in my life I was upset because a boy made racist jokes about my race and religion. He had an air of arrogance and continued to hurt those around him. I was a little taken aback at first, but I soon reached a point of strength and explained to him that he was wrong in judging others. He apologized the next day.[19]

An Asian American girl recalls,

A senior boy used to yell, "Where's my money, soldier?" at me whenever I walked by him, implying that because I was Asian, I was like a whore at a GI service station in Vietnam (which sprung probably out of prejudice and ignorance). I tried ignoring him until it was unbearable. I confronted him about it. He didn't really have an explanation, but ever since then he hasn't done it.[20]

GANGS

Gangs are cited as a major struggle by 37 applicants in Question 1 ("What do you think are the most important issues/struggles facing teenage girls today?"); in Question 2 ("What do you wish you could change about your school, related to these issues?") nine respondents (including of the same 37, above) wished for no more gangs in school.

Hispanic girls cite problems with gangs more than girls from any other group. The following set of responses from a suburban Milwaukee girl are typical.

Question 1: What do you think are the most important issues/struggles facing teenage girls today?

Rape, getting pregnant, and people hurting people.

Question 2: What do you wish you could change about your school related to these issues?

People hurting people and the gangs in my school.

Question 3: What is something that someone has said to you, that you wish they hadn't said?

Someone had told me to be in a gang. I said no. It was my sister who asked me. She told me if I didn't she wouldn't talk to me

continued

A handful of respondents claim they have earned new respect for challenging peers' thinking or behaviors. Explains a 16-year-old,

For the past three years, I've learned that people will respect you if you come out strong and tell them you want nothing to do with drugs or alcohol to be accepted by them. Many of my friends are addicted to smoking and alcohol and respect me for being there to encourage them to quit. Even though these friends have problems, they aren't the types of people who peer pressure you."[21]

A 14 year-old views herself as a "mentor" or teacher: "People will accept you even if you're different, as long as you teach them," she says.[22]

Answers that see "the real you" threatened by the crowd and in need of protection from group-sanctioned behavior are notably more characteristic of white and Asian American respondents than blacks and Hispanics. These answers generally indicate a solitary or atavistic view of the "real" self, detached from social interaction. They assume that girls derive strength from protecting their authentic individual or solitary self from peer insults and, to some extent, from being alone—"being themselves" rather than being part of the social group. Conversely, they identify peer relations as troubling because they sometimes seem to conceal or inhibit the true self.

White respondents more frequently cite peer pressure and fitting in socially as major struggles, and they more frequently propose to resolve those struggles by standing alone, or being truer to their individual selves. As a Salt Lake City respondent recommends, "Don't give a damn. Don't stick your neck out for no reason."[23]

Such strategies may equip these girls with a greater sense of control over their lives. By the same token, these atavistic strategies may lead to a feeling of estrangement from constructive or positive peer relations, alienation from the peers who seem to exert such influence over their lives, and a sense of identity disconnected from social or community contexts. For example, a higher per-

GANGS *continued*

anymore. I wish she didn't put it that way.

Question 4: What is something that you know that you think other girls your age need to know?

It is about the gangs. I was in a gang before and I thought it was cool to be in a gang. I thought they were my family and that they would always be there for me when I got in trouble, but they weren't. When one person in the gang gets caught up, they say her name or someone else's name. They say you did it or the other person did it. So eventually you and your "gang" will get caught up and you all will have a record for gang banging. 'cause we all got caught and now we have a record. Some of the other gangs got caught too and they have a record too. ...

Milwaukee, Wisconsin, #23, Hispanic, 1

centage of white girls answering Question 5 ("What would you like to learn from other girls your age?") "want to know" if other girls feel "alone" and if their female peers face the same problems that they do. Of 603 respondents answering Question 5, 77 (13 percent) wonder if other girls feel alone; of these, 44 percent are white and 31 percent are Hispanic. Only 5 percent of the African American sample want to know if other girls share their problems.

Girls who do voice the question pose it this way:

"I would like to know that other girls my age feel strong and independent too.... I would like to know that I'm not alone."[24]

"How many feel the loneliness I do?"[25]

"Are they stressing about the same things I am?"[26]

"Have they ever been apt to what I have? Do they feel the same as I?"[27]

"I would like to know from girls my age how many of them feel lost or alone in their daily lives. I would like to know if they ever feel lonely or if they feel that a huge part of their life is just empty and no matter what they try they cannot fill that void of empty space."[28]

"Esteem"/"Respect": "Take Pride in Yourself"

[Gilroy, California, #30, Hispanic, 15]

Widely cited 1991 research by AAUW on girls and adolescent "self-esteem" noted racial and ethnic differences in the reported drop in self-esteem that many girls suffer during adolescence.[29] This drop was not evident, for example, among African American girls. Summit participants' advice to their peers to have more confidence, "self-esteem," or faith in their goals shows similar racial differences. The 66 respondents who gave such answers to Question 4 ("What is something that you know that you think other girls your age need to know?") tend to use different terms and discourses according to race/ethnicity.

White respondents link the term "self-esteem" in these answers to the idea of being "happy with yourself." As a Salt Lake City respondent muses, other girls need "to have high self-esteem, and if you have that, then people won't get to you so much." "Self-esteem" describes a girl's view about herself as told to herself. As illustrated in this response, girls may view esteem as a way of arming or insulating themselves against damaging peer interactions by having an internal view of the self that is positive, strong, and upbeat.[30]

African American and Hispanic girls also occasionally use the term "self-esteem" but make more frequent use of the term "respect." Respect in these answers connotes not only a sense of self-pride—similar to "esteem"—but a *reciprocal* relation with peers and adults that involves having self-respect, conferring respect on others, and being *respectful.* "Respect," unlike "esteem," is not exclusively something an individual can feel about herself, but also a deference or status given to others, and a model for positive social interactions (as opposed to being "disrespected"). Respect, then, encompasses "how [girls] present themselves" to others, how they "carry themselves" in social situations, *and* how they feel about themselves. It entails knowing how to "respect themselves and others."[31]

Girls describe the consequences of not having self-respect or respect for others as mutual and reciprocal. An Illinois participant asks, for example, "If you know that you have respect for yourself, why do you use violence?" Another advises, "[Girls] need to respect themselves and

> *I have a lot of friends and I don't drink, smoke, do drugs or have sex. I am not thin or fat. I am not pretty or ugly. I do not do things because other people do them. I am me. Being yourself is a lot cooler than being someone else.*
>
> York, Pennsylvania, #25, white, 15

others. Everyone has feelings just like everyone else.... They treat other people bad because they feel bad about themselves."[32] These answers link a lack of self-respect with a lack of respectfulness socially, as demonstrated in violence and put-downs.[33]

Similarly, a Long Island respondent explains that the consequence of a lack of self-respect is a lack of respect from others:

Another person's opinion does not rule over your own. A person needs self-respect to get through life because without it, people will take advantage of you because you have no respect for yourself. So why should they have respect for you?[34]

Conversely, says a South Carolina respondent, girls "need to be shown respect like any adult would like to be shown" just as they "need to know how to show respect" and "speak their minds."[35]

"Doing Drugs Will Get You Nowhere in Life"

[Illinois, #15, black, 15]

....

Girls' concerns about peer pressure and related issues do not vary markedly by region. The answers of city girls and rural girls show no notable differences, although summit locations and format make it difficult to determine residency definitively. Responses concerning the use of illegal drugs are illustrative. One would expect that urban girls might mention drugs more frequently as a peer "issue or struggle," but summit responses do not bear this out.

A total of 288 respondents (40 percent) cite drugs (including alcohol) as a major issue or struggle. Hispanic girls cite it most frequently: The 95 who do account for 54 percent of Hispanic respondents. Whites are next, with mentions from 84 girls—42 percent of the white sample. Native Americans citing drugs number 18—or 37 percent of the Native American sample; African Americans number 74—or 32 percent of the African American sample; Asian Americans number 18—or 31 percent of the Asian American sample.[36]

The distribution of responses that cite drugs or alcohol is roughly proportionate to the urban/non-urban distribution in the sample overall. Of the 84 whites who mention drugs, 26 percent are from large urban areas, which is consistent with whites' urban/non-urban representation in the overall survey sample. Of the Hispanic girls who mention drugs, 32 percent are from urban areas, which is close to the 30 percent of urban Hispanic girls in the pool overall; finally, 32 percent of the African American drug responses are urban—a lower percentage than the 39 percent urban representation in the sample.

Although the public tends to view drugs as a scourge of urban schools and communities, in particular, girls' summit responses suggest that the problem does not respect city boundaries. Similarly, girls' summit responses suggest that school violence involving peers and gangs is not a disproportionately urban phenomenon:

There is a lot of pressure to have sex, drink, and do drugs, even in this suburban town.

Green Bay, Wisconsin, #86, white, 15

Urban girls cite school violence and school gang violence no more frequently than rural girls.[37]

"Standing Up Together":
Sisterhood and the Metaphors of Female Friendship

Effort, Pennsylvania, #14, white, 12

....

Question 6 on the summit application form asks girls, "What is your definition of 'sisterhood'?" The question invites girls to speculate about what an ideal or abstract relationship between girls and women would be and what other relations it would resemble. Their answers show that girls see sisterhood as a valuable, though heavy, bond with important differences by race/ethnicity.

On the surface, responses to Question 6 seem uniform and fairly repetitive. Girls characterize sisterhood in positive terms—across all age, racial, ethnic, and regional categories. Some respondents (97, or 14 percent) recognize it as a "coming together" or bonding between girls or women; others (150, or 22 percent) describe it as a relationship that stipulates unconditional loyalty.[38] Typically, girls elaborate loyalty as "sticking together" through "thick and thin," "no matter what." Sisterhood is also envisioned as a mutual protection society—"when females stick together and have each other's backs," in the words of a Philadelphia respondent.[39]

Girls of all groups also consistently identify "sisterhood" as a *consoling,* or comforting, relationship (157, or 23 percent). These responses portray sisterhood as "being there" for other girls when they are "down," listening to their problems (an 11-year-old calls it "the chain of sympathy"), and picking up the pieces after other problems erupt in their lives. Sisterhood, imagined as a bond of consolation, assigns female relationships a caregiving and care-taking status. "It's girls who see another friend or even someone they don't know crying, hurt, or anything—to comfort and be there for them," states a 14-year-old from Arizona. Sisterhood is "girls helping girls through tough situations," according to a Georgia girl, or "sisters helping sisters in time of need," in the words of a Detroiter.[40]

Strikingly, only 10 of the 676 respondents to Question 6 (and only one white respondent) characterize sisterhood in terms of pleasure, playful companionship, or fun. The few subscribers to this alternative vision define it as follows:

"All girls from all cultures and beliefs to be together and get along and laugh, and just enjoy ourselves ..."[41]

"You could tell them your problems and they will understand. Someone to have fun with ... "[42]

" ... to have fun with your girlfriends ... "[43]

Adolescent girls more readily associate "sisterhood" with commiseration than with camaraderie based on fun, according to summit responses.

Notwithstanding these similarities, some interesting differences emerge by race and ethnicity in the metaphors and concrete reference points girls select to elaborate the ideal of "sisterhood." These differences may point to sources of strong, resilient relationships in girls' lives, and/or they may reflect girls' various hopes for what they would most like to see in female relationships.

A much higher percentage of African American and Hispanic respondents (19 percent each) define "sisterhood" with reference to their actual sisters, kin relations, or other literal family bonds. A 12-year-old African American speaks of "someone who is there for you (blood or not) who cares for you like a real sister." Sisterhood, says another black girl, is "being in the position of sister to the community, family, and friends." A Hispanic respondent describes a "sisterly relationship with your girlfriends." A Native American talks of "blood-related siblings or extremely close friends." These answers use the literal role of sister in the family to model sisterhood among girls and women in social relations. "It is someone you can confide in as if they were your real sister," summarizes an Asian American girl. Only 9 percent of the Native American respondents and 5 percent of the white sample use a family metaphor to define sisterhood, and 14 percent (97 total) of the sample overall use a blood tie as a point of comparison for relations between female friends.[44]

Respondents in the white sample, meanwhile, more frequently use the metaphor of *friendship* to describe sisterhood—they view "sisterhood" as *someone,* in the singular, who acts as a "best friend." Fifty-nine white girls (30 percent of the Question 6 white sample) offer this interpretation, compared to 19 percent of the Native American respondents, 13 percent of the Asian American respondents, 10 percent of the Hispanic respondents, and 7 percent of the African American sample. For these girls, sisterhood connotes "shared feelings and ideas which create a friendship between girls", it means "to love one another and to always have a friend to lean on", and it means "a close 'girlfriend.'" These respondents envision sisterhood as a bond primarily between two: "It is someone you are close to and you believe in them and they will help you and you will help them," volunteers one respondent. Sisterhood, says another, is *"two* best friends that are really close to each other; to know each other very well."[45]

> *[Sisterhood requires us] to help out when girls or women need it, to guide and lead into the future, to be a good role model to all women.... Believe it or not, in someone's eyes you and me are role models, whether we like it or not.*
>
> Nassau/Suffolk Counties, New York, #3, Hispanic, 14

A third rendition of sisterhood, offered predominantly by white and Hispanic respondents, emphasizes the sharing of *secrets,* or the maintenance of confidences and trust. The 79 Question 6 responses (12 percent of the overall sample) framing their definitions this way include 19 percent of the white sample and 13 percent of the Hispanic sample, compared to 11 percent of Asian American respondents, 7 percent of Native American respondents, and 6 percent of black respondents. These responses underscore that sisterhood involves enough trust for girls to risk disclosing the "hidden" self or "tell people secrets without having the fear that they will tell someone else." Sisterhood, says a 14-year-old Ohio girl, is "where you get to know someone so well... that you can trust them with all [y]our secrets." Says a Pennsylvania respondent, it's a bond with "a girlfriend who you can always talk to and *even* share your deepest secrets with." The higher percentage of white respondents idealizing sisterhood as a relationship permitting the "true" self to emerge is consistent with the racial and ethnic differences in other questions. As described earlier, white summit participants, in particular, see peer relations as a threat to the true expression of self and often advise withdrawal into the self as a protection against the "herd" mentality of cliques.[46]

Also consistent with responses to other questions, the African American sample characterizes sisterhood as embracing the ideas of "respect among each other" and "getting along." Black respondents volunteer these attributes of sisterhood at almost three times the rate of white respondents: Out of 42 respondents describing such traits, 26 are African American, nine are white, four are Hispanic, and three are Native American. "All the sisters need to stick together and stop fighting over 'he say, she say,'" insists an African American girl from California, "'cause we are one." Agrees a white 14-year-old from the same state, sisterhood is "a pact between women of trust and understanding each other. It is definitely not jealousy and calling each other sluts."[47]

Thirty-two respondents—many from urban areas such as Philadelphia and Detroit—distinguish sisterhood as a specifically racial or interracial concept: The racial concept describes unity within a particular race (for example, "Sisterhood is African American females getting along and treating each other with the utmost respect that they deserve … to come together as one.… "). The interracial concept describes a unity across the races. It is "when girls of any age and race can get together without fighting or arguing …," or it is "making all colors come together and let[ting] out a lot of these things that's been on our chest for a long time and we learn about each other and rejoice … "[48]

Finally, few summit respondents define sisterhood as a bond to advance shared political or social goals, even though the word entered the popular lexicon as a description of the feminist movement in the late 1960s and early 1970s. Only 44 summit participants (6 percent of the Question 6 sample) define sisterhood as a predominantly *political* relationship, a "group of women joined together for some purpose, such as work or fellowship" or "a huge network of women who are not only a powerful force but an insuperable support system for each other." Asian American girls contribute 10 of those 44 responses: They constitute 19 percent of the Asian American Question 6 sample. In contrast, only seven white girls (4 percent of the white Question 6 sample) describe sisterhood as a primarily political bond.[49]

Girls who emphasize sisterhood's political dimension describe it in terms of power and strengths: Sisterhood, they say, exists among females who "help you fight your battles." It's a way of "interact[ing] with society; [it consists of] connections and networking between strong and dedicated females." A 14-year-old Hispanic respondent emphasizes the leadership aspects of

Have groups for girls and guys where they can talk about themselves.

Georgia, #13, white, 12

the bond: Sisterhood, she says, imposes a responsibility "to help out when girls or women need it, to guide and to lead into the future, to be at least a good role model to all women.... Yeah, I know—corny—but true. Believe it or not, in someone's eyes you and me are role models, whether we like it or not."[50]

Conclusion

....

Summit participants have more to say about peer relations than family relations. The attention they give to sometimes problematic relationships with boys and girls their own age reflects the increased importance of these relationships at this stage of respondents' lives. The degree to which girls see peer pressure as a problem in their lives varies by race and ethnicity, with white and Asian American girls most apt to find it troublesome. Strategies for dealing with peer pressure also reveal racial and ethnic patterns: More white and Asian American respondents withdraw from the crowd, even at the risk of loneliness. More black and Hispanic respondents remain loyal to the group but insist on redefining the terms of their relationship.

Girls' answers highlight the need to confront peer influence honestly in interventions against teenage drug use, sexual activity, or other behaviors: Getting alienated from or "abandoned" by peers does not appear a realistic option for many girls, who, when forced to choose between being "true" to themselves and "fitting in," say they are more apt to pick the latter. Girls ask, in other words, for more concrete and realistic guidance about how to "say 'no'" in a way that won't lose friends. Explains a 13-year-old, "when you're alone with your friends that are drinking, smoking, and doing drugs, saying 'no' would make you their enemy, so most girls give in and become addicted and then their life just falls apart." A Philadelphia respondent succinctly asks for "more ways to try to get out of things that you don't want to do, but don't want to be left out or called names."[51]

Finally, the choice many girls—especially white respondents—describe between being in the herd or being "themselves" speaks to a lack of *positive* peer pressure in their lives or of a sense of positive identity within a community or a social network. These girls seek relations with friends who would encourage rather than thwart their efforts to be "unique" or "individual." "Don't have cliques"—do away with them—recommends a Western New York participant, "by pairing people who aren't friends." Suggests a Kansas City, Missouri, girl, "Have peer helpers to get [girls] to be friends again."[52]

Although creating positive peer pressure or dismantling cliques may seem a lofty if not impossible goal for schools, some junior highs have initiated programs to do just that. These programs, led by guidance counselors or students themselves, foster "uncompetitive friendship," says sociologist Patti Adler. They include a "clique buster" program called the "Circle of Friends," designed by a student in Long Beach, California. The 1998 program involved 500 students in reaching out to other students. "They signed pledges to make every student feel important and valued, and wore friendship bracelets as a sign they were ready to help," wrote an observer.[53] "Clique busting," even in the inhospitable world of junior high, may not be as unachievable a goal as girls imagine.

• Girls' Messages and Action Ideas •

Notable Program

Expand DARE Program and Extend It Into High School

Carson City, Nevada: DARE needs to continue beyond fifth grade. [It is] easy at that age to say no, tough when you are in high school and associating with older kids 18 to 21.

St. Tammany Parish, Louisiana: DARE program.

Action Plans

Have Realistic Programs and Examples of the Dangers of Drugs

Puget Sound, Washington: Have former drug users share with kids, because kids won't listen to parents or teachers.

Green Bay, Wisconsin: DRUGS: We want real stories, not just "no." We want to hear/learn from people who have experienced the consequences of substance abuse. We listen most to peers.

Carson City, Nevada: Would like classes at school to be in-depth and serious and show real life problems and solutions of people who have abused drugs and alcohol.

Have High School Girls Mentor Junior High Girls and Junior High Girls Mentor Elementary School Girls

Jefferson County, Wisconsin: Have a panel of high school girls answering middle school girls' questions.

Huntingdon County, Pennsylvania: Stop "dumb" assemblies; real stories are more effective. Use older students to educate elementary-age students.

Toledo, Ohio: Adults need to be role models. Also consider that senior high girls can mentor junior high; junior high can mentor elementary, etc.

Have Counseling and Mentoring Services That Encourage Girls to Intermingle More

Puget Sound, Washington: Set up situations where students have to meet new people.

Kenosha, Wisconsin: Sports—Put men and women together on a team.

Have Mentoring/Counseling Groups Organized by Peers

Rhinelander-Northwoods, Wisconsin: Establish mentoring/counseling groups.

Carson City, Nevada: Need to have student liaisons, peer counselors, or student mentors identified for students to openly discuss things of concern. Kids will talk to kids before they will go to an adult.

Illinois: Have "help" places for those who need help so they won't be violent…Conduct self-defense classes.

Messages to Girls

Peer Pressure, Friends, and Drugs

Puget Sound, Washington: "Don't stay in your personal 'bubble.'"

Asheville, North Carolina: Peers can lessen the emphasis on beauty. Compliment each other on a variety of things, not just appearance. Recognize jealousy and attempt to support those who are confident instead of criticizing them....

Green Bay, Wisconsin: There's a big pull between being and liking yourself and fitting in.

Montgomery County, Maryland: "Get jealous or admiring thoughts out in the open."

Tampa, Florida: Encourage each other not to smoke, drink, or take drugs. Make it an "uncool" thing to do.

Messages to Adults

Peer Pressure, Friends, and Drugs

St. Tammany Parish, Louisiana: Identify and address the pressure points: why are students vulnerable to peer pressure (attention, wanting acceptance, etc).

Arizona: Send home letters to parents, school board, city officials, business leaders and media on summit outcome.

CHAPTER 4

"Taking School
Seriously":
Girls as Learners
and Students

From a 14-year-old's summit questionnaire:

Question 1: What do you think are the most important issues/struggles facing teenage girls today?

Girls are often afraid to speak their mind because they are self-conscious and think what they say would be wrong. Girls are the quiet ones in most of my classes because the boys are loud and prevent the girls from learning, and girls won't say anything.

Question 2: What do you wish you could change about your school, related to these issues?

Girls should be told that what they say matters and they are important. All people who want to learn should be in certain classes and the people who don't take school seriously should be in other classes so the people who want to learn can learn....

Massachusetts, #4, white, 14

How do girls envision themselves as learners and students? How do their peers, parents, and teachers—key players in the formal and informal school cultures—contribute to this role? How do race/ethnicity and sex interact to define or restrict the role of the "achiever"? Finally, what factors might invite *all* girls to see themselves as achievers?[1] Summit responses to several questions, cumulatively, show that teens' status as "learners" or "achievers" is socially defined, often according to race, ethnicity, and gender, and by peers as well as adults within school.

At stake in the social definitions of "achiever" are not only students' *feelings* about learning but, according to recent research, their achievement level as well. Harvard researchers in 1999 found that positive stereotypes, such as "Asians are talented in math and science," boost academic performance, while negative stereotypes can hinder the performance of "stigmatized groups, such as women and African- and Hispanic-Americans." Earlier research by Claude Steele of Stanford University similarly found a "stereotype threat" in performance. When students are placed in a situation in which a poor performance would support a stereotype of inferior abilities because of the student's ethnicity or gender, Steele discovered, then the student's performance suffers. Yet the Harvard research clarifies that students are "susceptible" to *positive* as well as negative stereotypes of their academic abilities: Hence, positive social identification of girls as "high achievers" or learners in nontraditional fields, for example, may enhance their performance.[2]

> *I wish people would not make comments about my report card when I receive straight A's.... My friends should be happy for me, not demean my accomplishments*
>
> Morristown, New Jersey, #1, white, 15

Summit participants interpret the question about how schools could be improved in terms of their relations to peers and, somewhat less frequently, to teachers, counselors, and other adults within the school. As this chapter will discuss, the human and social dimensions of school weigh heavily on girls' minds and ultimately affect their learning experience. Similarly, the role or identity of the "student" and "learner" in school is in large measure defined according to race/ethnicity and gender—by peers as well as adults. Summit responses suggest that social interactions, personal struggles, and sexual behavior—issues captured in the 1992 term "evaded curriculum"[3]—profoundly affect students' learning experience, but are often not addressed by schools.

Many recent education reform agendas miss these issues, too, instead focusing on what researcher Maxine Greene calls a "technical perspective." This perspective, she says, assumes "the school's main mission is to meet the national economic and technical needs" as gauged by tests and other measures of standards achievement. Responses from summit participants, however, suggest these "technical" areas can't be isolated from the social realm. Girls' accounts show that the formal dimensions of schooling interact powerfully with the social, cultural, and human aspects of school life and that these latter issues may contribute to school success or failure.[4]

"It's Not the School—It's the People in It"

[Mississippi #33, black, 14]

....

Of all the elements that make up the formal and informal school contexts, respondents react most strongly to the people—adults and teens—with whom they interact in the course of a school day: The largest percentage of responses to Question 2 ("What do you wish you could change about your school ... ?")—53 percent—focus on changing the people in the school rather than programs, curriculum, or policies. By "people," respondents mean their peers more often than their teachers or administrators.[5] "I would either like to change the people or their way of thinking," a 13-year-old characteristically recommends.[6]

[I wish people wouldn't say,] "That's a stupid idea." After hearing it many times, it undermines one's confidence.

West Virginia, #1, Asian American, 15

Summit participants' school wish lists cover a wide range of peer behavior. Less sexual harassment and more comfortable girl-boy relations (see Chapter 2) earn mentions from 113 (17 percent) of Question 2 respondents. Those looking for more regulation of peer interaction—more discipline, supervision, or school dress codes ("so everyone looks and feels the same")—account for an additional 49 responses (8 percent). Eighty-six of Question 2 respondents (13 percent) want to see less peer pressure (50), fewer cliques (22), or less gossip (14).[7]

White and Asian American respondents, in keeping with their more frequent mention of "peer pressure" as a major struggle in their lives, contribute disproportionately to this cluster of answers.[8] A white girl from Arizona says, "Our school has a lot of peer pressure and if you don't do things a certain way, people look down on you or possibly injure you. I think we should have more people on grounds to make sure this doesn't happen." Other participants similarly remark:

"I wish that everyone didn't follow someone else. Even the people who are followed follow someone."

"[Girls should] not worry so much about the way we look in school. [I would like] not to be ashamed of who we are or our identity."

"I wish I could change [it so] ... that kids accept you for who you are and not what you have done with a boy or other things like drugs."

"[I wish we would] not have a popular group."[9]

Another set of Question 2 responses wishes that students would be "nicer" and friendlier. " ... Make it a more peaceful environment where everybody is treated equally," urges an Asian American participant. Imagines a Georgia girl, "I wish that girls at my school would not hate all other girls." Girls also yearn for a school environment that is "not so judgmental" and a school where "everyone can get along and then these kinds of things [pregnancy, violence, harassment] would not happen." A 15-year-old in Montana wishes bluntly that there were "no stuck-up girls."[10]

While the public at large ranks violence, gangs, guns, and drugs high on the list of public school problems, summit participants give other issues higher priority. Question 2 respondents would sooner change harassment, cliques, hostile peer relations, gossip and rumors, and peer coercion than they would physical violence or fighting (36 total), drugs in school (26 total), or gang activity (9 total). A higher percentage of African American and Hispanic girls wishes, as one girl says, "to stop the violence and for the youth to learn how to respect each other." Of the nine comments about gangs, five are from Hispanic girls and two from Native Americans: A Minneapolis participant would like to change "girls joining gangs to show they are just as hard and ruthless as young teen boys in gangs." As other research has shown, student energy expended on peer tensions, conflicts, fights, and harassment in school—or abuse and violence in the home—ultimately impedes teens' abilities to concentrate and learn.[11]

School Issues and Struggles: Too Little Pressure/Too Much Pressure

Overall, 23 percent of the "major issue" answers mention a school-related struggle, be it "school" generally, fear of dropping out, or concerns and pressure about grades. A higher percentage of the Asian American sample cites school in general as a major issue (28 percent); other such responses show little variation by race or ethnicity.

Dropping out shows up as a disproportionate concern of Hispanic and Native American girls. Both of these groups mention the struggle against dropping out or a fear of dropping out more than do white girls (2) or Asian Americans

If the school refuses to let you learn what you deserve, go learn yourself.
Morristown, New Jersey, #6, Asian American, 14

(0).[12] This subgroup difference reflects a demographic reality: Hispanic girls

What Schools Could Do Better

Four Girls Offer Their Suggestions

I wish the school would provide more opportunities for more girls to join things and accomplish things to be proud of, which would boost their self-esteem. [It would be good] if school gave out awards in other areas than academics.

Morristown, New Jersey, #4,
Asian American, 16

To help develop each person in their own individuality, it would be nice if schools got students to experience classes and activities that weren't conventionally dominated by their own sex. For example, if more women went to computer programming or power tech, with more males [going] to child psychology and home economics. Schools have been really good about having students experience more variety in their classes like this, but each person could more easily develop themselves as an

face a dropout rate of 30 percent, which threatens to become more pronounced in the next century, and Native American students have lower high school completion rates than white, black, or Asian American students. It should be noted that these dropout rates may also reflect the higher percentage of very low-income Americans in the Hispanic and Native American populations.[13]

Asian American and white girls, meanwhile, cite "pressure to get good grades," or concerns about getting high grades, more frequently than African American, Hispanic, and Native American respondents. Nine percent each of the Asian American and white respondents cite concerns about grades: A white respondent from Massachusetts says, "Parents put tons of pressure on girls to get A's. Girls put pressure on themselves, too. Getting a C on a mid-term could end life."[14]

In contrast, only 1 percent (3) of the African American sample, 3 percent of the Hispanic respondents, and none of the Native American respondents mention grades or pressure to achieve.

What Schools Could Do Better continued

individual instead of as a role in society if this was done more extensively.

Puget Sound, Washington, #18, white, 17

The school should reward you for other actions, like volunteering. This would help [reduce] achievement struggles.

Puget Sound, Washington, #19, white, 15

I would have after-school or school-related activities, and have peer mediators "floating" around campus at all times.

Arizona, #34, white, 12

White respondents' greater concern about grades is consistent with answers to Question 2 ("What do you wish you could change about your school, related to these issues?), where whites offer 10 of the 19 responses that schools should give less work and put less pressure on students. As one white girl says, "I wish the teachers would not give out so much homework and study all in one night."[15]

The Formal School Culture: "Have Teachers Treat Us With the Same Respect as They Treat Males/Athletes"

[Bozeman, Montana, #47, no race or age given]

Through their actions, teachers, counselors, and administrators either reinforce girls' roles as students—or challenge them. Belittling girls' abilities imposes a particularly severe challenge. But girls recount few anecdotes (no more than 20), dispersed throughout their applications, of overtly sexist comments and practices from teachers, counselors, and administrators.

A few summit participants assert that girls and boys are taught differently, evidenced by teacher comments or classroom practices. A Salt Lake City respondent wishes "people would treat girls the same as boys in the classroom." She qualifies that "obviously, the treatment will be a little different, but not based on gender." A 12-year-old from Toledo admits, "I wish that I could change the way teachers favor the male population in our school." Finally, a central Floridian claims that "gender is also a barrier used to prevent girls from achieving their goals. I wish that teachers would stop seeing gender, and treat everyone as 'just' a human being."[16]

A handful of anecdotes recall sexist and racist comments by teachers in the classroom. These include the following:

"My math teacher said that we Mexicans couldn't learn and that we were stupid."

"My driver's education teacher once told the class that girls couldn't drive as well as men. This made me really angry because he was stereotyping all girls."[17]

About a dozen students, at different points on the questionnaire, describe the classroom climate as disruptive because of boys' behavior toward girls. An Illinois respondent complains about an unruly classroom characterized by sexual "horseplay," saying, "It is very hard to learn anything when you have guys in the back of the room yelling stupid things at you." A Massachusetts girl says,

In most classrooms, girls are the quiet, studious students. Their opportunity to learn is taken away when troublemakers—in my experience they have been boys—disrupt the class. Many girls are self-conscious of their ability in the classroom. Because of this insecurity, they don't want to contribute in class discussion or ask questions. This problem is a result of both the males and females in the class, and their intolerance and disrespect of ideas girls have.[18]

More prevalent in summit participants' comments about what they want changed at school are requests that teachers and counselors do more to foster girls' identities as students and successful learners— or help them navigate social currents in school. The 71 such responses account for 11 percent of the Question 2 sample. Racial and ethnic differences in the responses suggest that African American and Hispanic students may feel especially underserved by some of the formal resources in school. A higher percentage of African American respondents (13 percent), for example, request better, more interesting teachers

Classes need to be geared toward the strength of both sexes rather than having a dominant one.

West Virginia, #1, Asian American, 15

and classes or that "school [be] more challenging." This response compares to 8 percent of the Asian American respondents, 6 percent of the Hispanics, and 5 percent of the whites.[19]

Girls seeking more from their schools call for livelier instruction ("I just wish they would make learning fun."), more teacher attentiveness ("Be more alert with students—communicate."), and/or more teacher commitment ("I wish I could change teachers because half of them don't teach us. They really don't care if you learn or not as long as they make their money."). A Delaware summit participant confides,

I wish that the school could be more understanding. The teachers are out to break our spirit. A lot of times, things are made as hard as possible to 'prepare you for the real world.' The preparation we need is the support to get emotional stability so we can function in the "real world."[20]

A Washington, D.C., respondent castigates teachers who are overly critical of students: "I wish that teachers didn't put you down to the point that you can't concentrate on getting your grades up before you make the choice of dropping out."[21]

Hispanic girls account for 12 of the 19 requests for better counselors in school—a request made by only four white and three African American respondents.[22] These Hispanic girls may believe that counselors—typically overextended—have unique potential to help them navigate school. Or the girls may have had more negative or unproductive experiences with counselors and thus flag them as an underutilized resource in school. A Hispanic respondent conceives, for example, of a school where "there would actually be someone that we could actually talk to about [issues] and maybe even get some real advice."[23]

> *I always wish that people hadn't always referred to me as brilliant because they teased me horribly. They also tried to become my friend for better grades.*
>
> Nassau/Suffolk Counties, New York, #82, Hispanic, 12

In some cases, summit participants report that counselors curtail their ambitions: A black girl from Philadelphia relates,

> I wish the counselors never said that we need to apply to CCP [Community College of Philadelphia] because of our financial standing and that if we want to pursue a career in law, we should consider being a paralegal. This made me feel like she

only had small expectations of minority students that attended an inner city school, in an area people consider the "ghetto."[24]

The Informal School Culture: "Girls [Should Not Be] Persecuted for Their Intelligence"

[Massachusetts, #1, Asian American, 15]

....

Peers, however, draw more blame than teachers or counselors for discouraging school achievement. Summit participants, in various areas of the questionnaire, recall substantially more incidents of peers delimiting their role as students or "smart girls" than teachers or counselors. Descriptions of these negative encounters show the tension many girls feel between school achievement and peer approval. As an Asian American respondent explains, "Teenage girls feel pressure to do well in school *while* trying to fit in." Doing well, in other words, competes against "fitting in."[25]

Indeed, summit participants outline a repertoire of ways that their peers restrict the value and social prestige of traditional academic achievement. In response to Question 3 ("What is something that someone has said to you that you wish they hadn't said?"), 130 (21 percent) of the respondents recall someone's belittling their ambitions, insulting their intelligence, accusing them of being a "teacher's pet," mocking them as racial imposters because of their achievements (that is, "acting white"), or challenging girls' abilities in general.

A higher percentage (8 percent) of white than other respondents to Question 3 recount incidents in which boys belittled girls as a sex generally. For example, one recalled hearing, "Boys are better than girls. It was a boy that said this." Another reported being stung by the words,

"You're just a girl, though. Rise above the female stereotype!" A third says she is tired of hearing, " 'She can't because she is a girl.' This happens often." These girls are either more often the audience for generic sexist comments, or they are more affected by such statements. Among non-white respondents, only three—an Asian American, a Hispanic, and a Native American—recount a generic sexist comment in this question.[26]

In contrast, 53 girls (9 percent of the Question 3 sample) tell of having personally been called "stupid" or intellectually incompetent. Of these girls, 22 (42 percent) are Hispanic. Only eight white students (4 percent of the white sample), three Asian American (6 percent of the Asian American sample), and three Native Americans (9 percent of the Native American respondents) report having been intellectually belittled personally, in comparison to 14 percent of the Hispanic respondents.

Someone said, "Are you in special education?" because I didn't understand something.

Ann Arbor, Michigan, #20, black, 15

"Someone once told me that I was not smart enough to get good grades and succeed," one Hispanic girl writes, "because that day I failed my math test and started to cry. But that is not true because I am smart and even smart people can make mistakes." African Americans are also over-represented in this group, with 17 responses (9 percent of the African American sample). "People thought I was retarded," recalls an African American student. A few respondents recollect that their parents insulted their intellectual ability: A white girl from Brainerd, Minnesota, writes, "I wish my stepmother never would have said, 'You're not the smart person in the family, so stop answering my question.'").[27]

Notwithstanding the ubiquity of hurtful comments and social judgments in adolescent life, it is intriguing that some racial and ethnic patterns emerge in the sorts of stories and aspersions that girls recall as especially profound. Different groups of girls may either encounter certain forms of ridicule more often than others, probably according to ethnic and racial stereotypes, or they may simply find particular kinds of insults especially troubling or memorable—again, perhaps according to their own understanding of racial and ethnic stereotypes. (For example, a Hispanic girl who senses that peers doubt her academic ability may recall more vividly actual incidents where that ability was insulted; alternately, her peers may exploit the available stereotypes of Hispanic students as fodder for social insults.)

A clear nexus of race and gender emerges around the taunts of "acting like a white girl," "acting white," or "sounding like a white girl," cited in Question 3 by nonwhite girls as stinging accusations designed to punish or belittle their academic engagement. In these examples, girls' academic identity is cast as a "white" trait or characteristic, such that those nonwhite girls who claim academic interests and success as their own are traitors to their race. A Hispanic girl recalls, "Someone said that I thought that I was all that and I think I'm better than everyone else. And I am a disgrace to the Spanish people." "Achievement" by this logic becomes the property of white girls and a source of social censure for nonwhite learners. As a Native American laments, "You can't imagine how much I've been criticized for reading."[28]

High-achieving girls of all races and ethnicities also report having been taunted as "over-achievers," sellouts, or "teacher's pets." Some girls recall incidents where their intellectual, academic, and sexual identities were critiqued simultaneously and mutually. For example, they may report that they were called a "bitch" or a cold fish *because* they were too successful or committed to academic and other achievement goals. A York County, Pennsylvania, respondent states, "A lot of people consider me a *bitch,* because I strive to achieve my goals, because I'm not afraid to lead, and I'm very independent, and my goals are painfully important to me." An Indianapolis 12-year old volunteers that "someone said that I was too brainy *and I don't like boys.*"[29]

In these stories, girls' intellectual achievement gets recast as a sign of diminished heterosexuality or femininity, or of "bitchiness." A Willimantic, Connecticut, participant describes having been "called a slut" for being assertive. She continues, "When I asked him why, he said, 'Because you're really hyper and proud.' This pisses me off." A 15-year-old Asian American expresses eloquently the struggle to be a good student while simultaneously finding a way to "fit in":

> *I think we should leave the boys alone and just do our work.*
> Detroit, Michigan, #18, black, 12

> By my peers I am considered one of the good/smart kids. Many see me in this light and respect it, but there is that small group that takes the positive intelligence of my friends and myself and turns it into a negative.... I would like to change the turning of the positive into a negative, so that intelligent girls are not persecuted for their intelligence.[30]

Despite the threat of social ridicule, African American girls predominate among respondents who advise their peers to care more about school. Out of 52 such responses, 27 (53 percent) are from African American girls.[31] "People in school should come to school and learn, not gang bang and other things that don't have anything to do with school," urges an Illinois participant. "School is the most important thing [girls] have," counsels a Hispanic respondent, "not guys, drugs, etc."[32]

Similarly in answers to Question 2, more African American girls speculate that their school would be improved if students were more serious about learning and education: Of such responses, nine out of 17 came from African American students. These girls wish, for example, "that peers would encourage you to be smart and succeed in school." None of the white sample envisions this improvement.[33]

Notably, many of the same African American and Hispanic respondents who want girls to be more serious about learning describe sex and pregnancy as impediments to this goal in their Question 2 and Question 4 responses. A Hispanic girl reminds her peers, "School is where you get an education,

All the hate that people show towards one another is really sad. People are sooo mean these days.

Bozeman, Montana, #44, no race or age given

not boyfriends." In three different cities, three black and Hispanic 13-year-olds give the following advice:

"Girls need to get their education before having sex."

"[Girls need to know] not to get pregnant, and get an education."

"All girls my age think about is boys. Some may know that education is important, but some may not."[34]

As common sense would predict, these responses construe pregnancy, sexual relations, and school achievement as intermeshed, despite a tendency in much social and political policy to treat them as discrete problems.[35]

Reimagining School: "I Wish School Was a Place Where People Encourage You to Resist Your Struggles"

[Auburn, California, #2, Asian American, 16]

....

The overwhelming majority (92 percent) of all respondents can think of at least one change schools could make to help students along. Girls' blueprints for better schools reveal fewer racial and ethnic differences than other responses.

But girls' answers do fall across a spectrum. At the most cynical end, 23 students (4 percent) feel schools can do nothing to help teens with their issues and struggles. Schools, they say, are incapable of helping because "if teens want to do something bad enough they will"; because "the schools don't control kids, no matter how hard they try"; or because the struggles they face are "mostly a fact of life. The school you go to can't control this. Only you can."[36]

At the most optimistic end of the spectrum, another 4 percent of respondents—24 total—state that they would not want to change their school because it is doing a good job and they are proud of it. Notably, a higher percentage of urban than suburban participants cite pride in their schools. What do these schools do right? Some girls report that students in their schools do not have serious problems; other participants who cite pride in their schools describe specific characteristic or programs that make them work. Typically, some of the programs and attitudes that girls praise combine the social and educational aspects of schooling. "I don't wish I could change anything about my school," a Detroit participant wrote. "Actually, I'm proud of my school because of the young parent program they have here. It helps the young mothers at Murray stay in school."[37]

Other effective schools appear to knit together educational, social, or personal issues through the use of counselors, social workers, and support groups or classes: "There is a course in our school for girls and we talk about those [personal] issues and many more," says a Philadelphia girl. Two respondents attribute their schools' effectiveness to the fact that the schools are small and less clique-oriented, or more able to consider personal and academic problems together. "My school is very small ..." says a California respondent, "so these aren't really issues there."[38]

These characteristics of the effective school resonate in other girls' visions of what could be better in their schools. Many of the "school change" answers to Question 2 describe worlds in which there is (a) more openness, communication, discussion, or support for social and personal problems in school (111 total answers) and (b) a fusing of the social support system with the academic support system. While many policy and reform debates treat the school's academic and social functions as wholly distinct spheres, summit participants experience school as a totality that includes both these aspects. Girls may experience school even more acutely as

[I wish] that the school would not be so afraid to get involved and do something about issues.

West Central, Montana, #2, white, 17

a social milieu because they face more pressure to conform to sexual and social norms.[39] Summit responses show girls want to attend a school that recognizes and grapples with the interdependency of academic and social worlds, so that the school is "more personalized and not so militaristic and you weren't just a number." A 14-year-old writer describes this interdependency: "I wish that there could be a program at all schools about teen pregnancies and other problems. These problems don't only occur outside of school so we need programs at school because this is where they occur."[40]

Girls propose meshing school academics and social support by calling, in some cases, for teachers, counselors, and other adults to function as personal advisors as well as educational mentors. A Delaware girl, for example, envisions a school where conversation could move easily between personal and academic challenges: "We should be able to pick our favorite teacher that understands me better. Have a group in school and all of us get together after school and do our homework and talk about home and health problems." The fluidity of academic and social resolutions to problems is also clear in a response from Green Bay, Wisconsin:

I wish teachers would be more open to those students who do bad in school. Some of them get so much pressure and they want to fit in a group so much that they do stupid things. If a teacher befriends one of their students, the student might be able to know that someone cares and take their lives more seriously. When people think no one cares, they do things that they wouldn't do otherwise.[41]

This participant sees a teacher's responsiveness to students who are faring badly academically in school as a way to help them in their *personal* struggles and vice versa: Attention to academic problems will help students "take their lives more seriously" so that they will not do "stupid things" socially just to fit in with a group.

Finally, a Kenosha, Wisconsin, respondent recommends a "special class throughout the week where girls could go and talk about issues with teachers/counselors, and maybe share experiences if they feel comfortable doing so."[42]

Some respondents suggest ways that schools could better combine personal, social, and academic concerns. One proposes giving peers more opportunities to assume the "adult" roles of counselor and teacher to one another. Such responses challenge the traditional "adult"/educator and "student"/learner dichotomy. Says one respondent, "[Schools need] more study groups in the classes, and programs organized by students." A South Dakota respondent thinks schools would be better if "we could have a mediation process for girls and boys that is *set up* by the girls and

> *I wish our school could change our [tutoring] program into a program where we can discuss these issues [pregnancy, STDs, intercourse].*
>
> Detroit, Michigan, #5, black, 12

boys." A Philadelphia girl endorses a similar idea of using peers to help mediate disputes: Disputes could be resolved faster, she says, "if [peers] can have meetings with a couple of students to see what's going on, instead of the girls/boys coming up to the counselor," something, she says, "they sometimes are afraid to do."[43]

Despite some critics' recent claims that girls have usurped educators' attention, to boys' detriment, summit participants feel schools do not pay *enough* attention to social issues, especially those involving gender roles. Respondents see attempts to confine gender roles as detrimental to their well-being in school as well as to the learning environment overall. Some girls (25, or 4 percent) suggest that single-sex classes might help with this problem. Others feel that the school neglects *girls* specifically: Says a Minneapolis respondent, "I wish girls would be recognized as an issue. Many refuse to deal with the simple fact that there is a problem and continue to punish instead of offering some solutions." More respondents, however, (52 total) argue that schools need to "be more aware of what is happening" in a general sense. "Don't ignore issues like [sex] that are real and happen every day," urges a Long Island respondent. A Midwesterner similarly pleads, "I wish I could make the schools more understanding, aware, and caring to notice the problems and then try to care enough to stick with things, until they are solved." Finally, a Green Bay, Wisconsin, respondent criticizes "the ways that the school walks around problems. I wish they would just come out and say what's going on."[44]

The call for greater awareness, openness, or involvement is intriguing, since most schools do pay some attention to sex and health education in the formal curriculum or through support groups. Yet responses to Question 2 recommend not more *information* but, rather, more *involvement* by educators and other adults in the social or nonformal aspects of school life. It is important to see the two as distinct characteristics. More involvement and awareness demand an understanding of the social tensions that underlie and compound student risks, and a willingness to address that subtext effectively. These girls are envisioning a different *sort* of attention to the issues that affect their school lives.

What would that attention look like? Forty-nine respondents recommend more sex education programs; 59 call for more "rap sessions" or support groups. More specifically, they want programs "where they told more than just the facts that you should use a condom when having sex." These classes, as idealized in Question 2 responses, would move beyond "just learning the cold facts" and get to the issues behind sex and pregnancy. A 17-year-old from Illinois wants, for example, "someone at our school to consult with about sex." A peer in another part of the state wants not a class on pregnancy prevention or birth control, per se, but a "sexuality class for kids to express their feelings." Girls want more than objective data; they want to learn more about the feelings, choices, and issues that underlie risks such as drugs or pregnancy in their lives.[45]

> *we need more clubs to join where you could easily get to know your fellow classmates and prove to them that you are a trustworthy friend.*
>
> Minneapolis, Minnesota, #49,
> no race or age given

Conclusion

....

Summit responses show that girls experience the academic and social worlds of school as intertwined and idealize school services that would address both areas simultaneously. Education reformers who focus on standards, school accountability, testing, and other formal mechanisms for stimulating greater school achievement may find that these reforms fail if the human, social, and cultural aspects of school life—which shape students' identity and experiences in school—are not transformed, in some way, at the same time. Anecdotally, girls recommend some innovative and strong strategies for improving school culture. Some girls propose support systems and groups that address academic and personal problems jointly: Such groups may be especially beneficial for Hispanic girls, whose prohibitive high school dropout rate is linked strongly to teen pregnancy.[46] Other girls suggest that peers play a more prominent role as mediators and counselors to alleviate social tensions in school. Hispanic girls, especially, recommend that counselors and the counseling system be better resourced to help them navigate school life. African American girls, particularly, ask for more interesting teachers and a more serious academic environment.

A bigger challenge will be recognizing the ways gender expectations shape school climate. More generally, many girls write that their conflicts in school play out as gender conflicts: Peers and adults police gender barriers, effectively defining who can learn and who will win or lose approval.

• Girls' Messages and Action Ideas •

Action Plan
....

Students Should Mentor Other Students

Willimantic, Connecticut: We want peer leadership/education. Middle school kids teaching elementary ... high school kids teaching middle school.

Have More Summits or Summit Groups in School

Toledo, Ohio: We should have summit groups like this in *school.*

Covina, California: Interested teacher paid to have a Saturday summit with chat rooms with girls.

Teachers Should Be More Involved in Our Lives and More Observant

Carson City, Nevada: Teachers need to get involved with students in order to watch out for rude comments that lower self-esteem.

Savannah, Georgia: "Teach school administrators to CARE about US."

Teachers Need Training About Students' Lives, How to Handle Gender Bias and/or Harassment

Wilmington, North Carolina: Educate educators about what students really think and need.... Much more discussion is needed between teachers and students. Conflict mediation needs to be taught and practiced in schools.

Tampa, Florida: Train teachers on gender and racial discrimination and enforce the consequences if they discriminate.

Have More Interesting Classes and Lessons

Willimantic, Connecticut: We want more expressive and creative ways to learn.

Delaware: Be stricter about curriculum: Teacher should provide interesting lessons not just read out of the book and answer the questions.

Other School Action Plans

Kenosha, Wisconsin: Students identified what behaviors help them to be successful and what traps or obstacles impede their success. We role-played classroom situations where students who underachieve impact the classroom and attitudes towards learning. Sisters then found solutions or methods to handle those behaviors, both as a classroom participant and as teachers. Handouts were also given so sisters could identify their learning styles.

Wisconsin: Schools for the 21st century. In our vision of the 21st-century, schools should have equity, concern for class size, discipline: Class size— room to spread, more opportunities to participate, quieter, easier to have questions answered (more one-on-one help).

Allentown, Pennsylvania: Schools should offer on-site professional day care to help teen moms stay in school. Home schooling should be an option for girls who cannot be in school. The teen mothers may also need foster care for teen mom and baby.

Messages to Girls

Tampa, Florida: Congratulate each other on academic achievement.

Messages to Teachers and Other Adults

Tampa, Florida: Encourage girls to achieve in school, to go on to further education or to seek out nontraditional, high-wage jobs.

Appendixes

• Appendix A—Parameters of Research •

This is a qualitative, interpretive study of roughly 2,100 girls' responses—from more than 50 locations nationwide—to six questions posed in 1997 and 1998 on AAUW's Sister-to-Sister summit application form. The questions were:

1. What do you think are the most important issues/struggles facing teenage girls today? [name three to five]

2. What do you wish you could change about your school, related to these issues?

3. What is something that someone has said to you that you wish they hadn't said? [give background and circumstances, if appropriate]

4. What is something that you know that you think other girls your age need to know?

5. What would you like to learn from other girls your age?

6. What is your definition of "sisterhood"?

The AAUW Educational Foundation crafted these questions in conjunction with education scholar Michelle Fine of the City University of New York to learn girls' views of their lives and to gain a deeper understanding of the subtleties behind the dry general statistics on education, gender, and adolescence today. AAUW branches occasionally modified these questions slightly, or asked girls a seventh question concerning what the community could do to help them with their struggles. Not all branches that sponsored summits asked these questions.

The report is based on a close reading and analysis of the responses from girls registering for a summit; applications were received by the AAUW Educational Foundation prior to December 1, 1998.

A subsample of 737 respondents was coded and analyzed using NUD*IST software for qualitative projects. This subsample includes all summit responses from the original 2,100 received before December 1, 1998, from all girls who identified themselves as Hispanic (185 total), Asian American (57 total), and Native American (50 total).

Undoubtedly, more girls of these ethnicities participated in actual summits, but they did not identify their race/ethnicity on the application form, or their demographic information was not included with their written responses.

Because African American and white summit participants were too numerous to code every response extensively, a random sample of these two groups was included in the database. Out of a pool of more than 500 African Americans and 650 whites, 233 African American and 212 white responses were included in the sample. In summits with 11 or fewer African American or white participants, every application was coded; in summits with 11 or more African or white participants, one-third of the responses from each of these two groups were pulled randomly and coded. Only those applications with demographic information on race/ethnicity and age, and applications with at least two questions answered, were eligible to be included in the African American and white samples.

The ages of most of the roughly 2,100 summit participants whose responses formed the basis of this report were 13, 14, or 15 years old. In the smaller coded sample of 737 girls, the age distribution was as follows:

Age 11	44 girls	(6 percent of the sample)
Age 12	153 girls	(21 percent of the sample)
Age 13	173 girls	(23 percent of the sample)
Age 14	130 girls	(18 percent of the sample)
Age 15	112 girls	(15 percent of the sample)
Age 16	61 girls	(8 percent of the sample)
Age 17	24 girls	(3 percent of the sample)
Age not given	40 girls	(6 percent of the sample)

Regionally, the summit database drew in roughly equal numbers from all sections of the United States. The largest percentage (34 percent) of summit questionnaires were submitted by girls living in the Midwest region. Twenty percent (20 percent) came from the West/Northwest region. The remainder of the questionnaires was distributed fairly evenly among the Mid-Atlantic (15 percent), the Southeast (15 percent), the Southwest (8 percent), and the Northeast (8 percent).

In terms of summit participants' urban, rural, or suburban origins, roughly one in three (31 percent) of the summit applications included in this report were drawn from summits held in major metropolitan areas. Such sites included Detroit, Philadelphia, Tampa, Salt Lake City, Washington, D.C., Milwaukee, Seattle, Buffalo (New York), Cleveland, and Long Island. This number does not include statewide summits—likely to have drawn from a variety of communities within the state—or summits held in communities such as Cobb County, Georgia, or Orange County, California, that constitute part of a larger metropolitan region or area.

Selecting a subsample for analysis using NUD*IST was especially recommended by the high level of thematic repetition in answers among respondents participating in the same summits. Sample percentages were tested on a few points against the summit responses in total to confirm their similarity. Because all 737 girls in the subsample did not answer every one of the six study questions, there are slight variations, from question to question, in the number of responses upon which percentages are based.

As cautioned in the introduction, *Voices of a Generation* is a qualitative research report, and its percentages and numbers are not reliable to "predict"or generalize about statistically significant differences between populations. An inferential statistical study, in contrast, would involve a representative sample of various populations of girls, and would generate data that could be considered predictive of an entire population. It would note statistically significant differences between groups with a high level of confidence.

The report also allows for possible differences in the *contexts* of summit participants' responses. Girls may have interpreted the six questions in different ways: Some girls may be describing problems that they think are faced by teens in general, and some may be describing problems that they experience personally. Some girls may have answered the questions in private, while others may have authored answers collectively, or in the presence of peers. Finally, although the vast majority of girls completed application forms weeks prior to the summit, some girls may have completed application forms on the day of the summit. Responses completed on the day of a summit may have been influenced by chat room topics or especially influenced by conversations with friends also attending the summit. These different contexts for girls' narratives should be kept in mind as the responses are discussed and reproduced in this report.

Throughout the report, speakers are identified by their summit site (for example, Tampa or Philadelphia), assigned study number, race/ethnicity, and age; in rare cases, only partial information is available. Readers should use caution in drawing inferences about summit participants based on urban, rural, or other characteristics of the summit sites. In some cases, neighboring cities or towns collaborated in hosting a summit, but gave that summit a single place name. Also, as noted in the acknowledgments, some host sites drew girls from broad surrounding areas. In the most extreme case, the Minneapolis summit involved girls from Minneapolis, Duluth, St. Paul, Rochester, and Red Wing. The Willimantic, Connecticut, summit drew girls from Storrs, Willimantic, the Middletown metropolitan area, and the lower Connecticut Valley.

• APPENDIX B—SISTER-TO-SISTER SUMMITS •

The following is a list of AAUW's Sister-to-Sister Summits and the dates on which they took place. In most cases, summit names are identical to the names of the AAUW Branches and States that sponsored them. Where they are not, the names of sponsors appear in parentheses after the summit name. Not all summits contributed to this report. For more information about the summits, see the introduction and Appendix A.

Branches

ALABAMA
Auburn, 4/4/98
Birmingham, 11/8/97
Huntsville, 4/18/98
Mobile, 4/25/98

CALIFORNIA
Auburn, 1/31/98
Benicia-Vallejo, 11/14/98
Covina, 7/1/98
Gilroy, 10/24/98
Laguna Beach, 10/3/98
Orange County Interbranch Council,
    10/24/98
Palo Alto, 10/24/98

CONNECTICUT
Norwalk-Westport & Bridgeport, 11/7/98
Willimantic (Storrs-Willimantic, Lower
    Connecticut Valley, & Greater
    Middletown), 6/13/98

DISTRICT OF COLUMBIA*
Washington, D.C. (Centennial), 4/18/98

FLORIDA
Central Brevard County, 10/3/98
Citrus County, 9/19/98

Pensacola, 11/10/98
Tampa, 1/19/98

GEORGIA
Cobb County, 5/16/98
Roswell-Alpharetta, 3/14/98
Savannah, 9/19/98
Valdosta, 3/21/98

ILLINOIS
Aurora, 5/20/98
Barrington Area, 5/16/98
Moraine Valley, 7/25/98

INDIANA
Anderson, 11/21/98
Ft. Wayne, 9/26/98
Gary-Merrillville, 5/26/98
Indianapolis, 2/28/98

IOWA
Marshalltown, 10/3/98
Vinton, 4/25/98

KANSAS
Salina, 2/26/98

LOUISIANA
St. Tammany Parish (Covington-Mandeville),
    10/24/98
Metairie-East Bank & New Orleans,
    11/10/98

*For AAUW organizational purposes, Puerto Rico and Washington, D.C., are accorded the same status as states.

MARYLAND
Montgomery County Interbranch Council, 3/28/98

MICHIGAN
Ann Arbor, 4/25/98
Detroit, 1/23/98 & 4/28/98
Port Huron, 9/12/98

MINNESOTA
Brainerd, 10/3/98
Minneapolis, 4/2/98

MISSISSIPPI
Oxford, 3/28/98

MISSOURI
Kansas City North (Missouri AAUW, Liberty, Richmond, Kansas City Northland, Northern Clay County, Parkville), 2/28/98
Kansas City South (Belton, Independence, Kansas City, Raytown), 11/14/98
St. Louis (Ballwin-Chesterfield, Creve Coeur, Ferguson-Florissant, Kirkwood-Webster Groves, St. Louis, St. Charles), 10/17/98

MONTANA
Bozeman, 3/07/98
Kalispell, 4/18/98

NEVADA
Carson City, (Capital), 3/28/98
Reno, 5/9/98

NEW JERSEY
Central NJ, 10/16/98
Morristown, 5/2/98
Northern NJ, 10/30/98
Southern NJ, 10/28/98

NEW MEXICO
Belen, 11/6/98

NEW YORK
Cortland, 11/14/98
Long Island Interbranch Council, 11/6/98
Northern Westchester, 10/24/98
Western NY (NY AAUW, Amherst, Buffalo, East Aurora-Southtowns), 3/28/98

NORTH CAROLINA
Asheville, 5/2/98
Gaston Regional, 10/17/98
Greensboro, 3/28/98
Hendersonville, 9/26/98
Wilmington, 7/12-18/98

OHIO
Bellefontaine, 4/4/98
Cincinnati, 10/24/98
Cleveland, 4/25/98
Toledo, 4/4/98
Youngstown, Boardman-Canfield, 10/29/98

OREGON
Baker City, [4 mini-summits took place in fall/winter '98]
Ontario, 4/4/98
Roseburg, 10/10/98

PENNSYLVANIA
Allentown, 11/14/98
Fox Chapel Area, 10/10/98
Huntingdon, 10/9/98
Bucks County (Levittown-Lower Bucks & Makefield Area), 11/14/98
Philadelphia, 11/15/97
Effort (Pocono Area), 5/16/98
York, 10/17/98

PUERTO RICO*
San Juan, 11/7/98

SOUTH CAROLINA
Beaufort, 11/24/98
Greater Columbia, 4/18/98

SOUTH DAKOTA
Rapid City, 5/6/98

TEXAS
El Paso, 10/17/98
Lubbock, 4/25/98

UTAH
St George, 10/24/98
Salt Lake City, 10/24/98

VIRGINIA
Newport News, 1/31/98
Northern Virginia Interbranch Council,
    11/7/98
Virginia Beach, 11/7/98

WASHINGTON
Puget Sound Area (7 branches), 5/9/98

WISCONSIN
Eau Claire-Menomonie, 11/14/98
Jefferson County (Ft. Atkinson, Whitewater,
    Watertown), 3/7/98
Green Bay Area, 5/5/98
Janesville, 9/26/98
Kenosha, 7/25/98
Suburban Milwaukee (North Shore-
    Milwaukee, West Suburban Milwaukee),
10/31/98
Rhinelander-Northwoods, 11/14/98

States

Arizona 10/24/98 & 5/8/98
Delaware, 2/21/98
Illinois, 7/25/98
Massachusetts, 5/2/98
Mississippi, 7/11/98
North Carolina, 11/21-22/98
South Carolina, 3/27/98
West Virginia, 3/28/98
Wisconsin, 11/7/98

Endnotes

Chapter One

....

1. John Gray's pop psychology work, *Men Are From Mars, Women Are From Venus: A Practical Guide for Improving Communication* (New York: HarperCollins, 1992) posits what researcher Barbara Kerr calls the "myth that men and women are so alien to one another that they can get along only by using intricate strategies of manipulation." See Barbara Kerr, "When Dreams Differ: Male-Female Relations on Campus," *Chronicle of Higher Education,* 5 March 1999.

2. Because there were more white and Asian American girls in the 17- and 18-year-old age brackets, these racial groups are overrepresented in this chapter, which draws mostly from analysis provided by older high school students. Additionally, however, it is probable that white girls may be more deeply troubled by or attuned to the cues from the "media" because, with notable exceptions, the fashion industry, teen magazines, and television programs exhibit predominantly white, female images. Nonwhite girls, perhaps because they are less likely to see their race represented in the media, may ironically be less preoccupied or negatively influenced by the body images and constricting aesthetic standards of popular media.

3. "I would like to know ..." [Salt Lake City, Utah, #32, white, 14]
   "I'm only 16 years old but ..." [Philadelphia, #17, black, 16]

4. "I want to know how to live ..." [Mississippi, #21, white, 13]
   "not a kid/not an adult." [Kalispell, Montana, #40, white, 13]
   "to stop putting kids in an adult role ..." [South Carolina, #8, black, 13]
   "the media sells images ..." [Auburn, California, #25, Asian American, 18]

5. Emphasis (italics) in quotes from girls, here and throughout this report, is the author's, unless otherwise specified as emphasis that the applicant used herself.

6. "find the person she really is" [Green Bay, Wisconsin, #72, white, 15]
   "pressure to be somebody they're not ..." [Kalispell, Montana, #52, white, 16]
   "struggle against conformity ..." [Massachusetts, #3, white, 15]
   "what a society expects girls to be ..." [Ann Arbor, Michigan, #5, black, 17]

7. "Girls struggle the most to fit in ..." [Massachusetts, #11, white, 13]
   "There are hundreds of kids ..." [Carson City, Nevada, #20, no age or race given]
   Patricia Hersch, *A Tribe Apart: A Journey Into the Heart of American Adolescence* (New York: Fawcett Books, 1998).

8. "outside forces ..." [Massachusetts, #7, Asian American, 15]
   "I wish that I could change ..." [South Dakota, #4, white, 15]
   "Society needs to change ..." [South Dakota, #4, white, 15]
   "a struggle to truly find ourselves ..." [Puget Sound, Washington, #18, white, 17]

9. "While times are changing ..." [Illinois, #95, white, 15]
   "didn't have to always be so self-independent ..." [Delaware, #9, white, 15]
   "a clearer, more realistic definition ..." [Auburn, California, #20, white, 17]

10. "teen magazines, like *Teen* or *YM* ..." [California, #7, white, 16]
    "abusive pop music ..." [Toledo, Ohio, #8, black, 12]
    "TV, which sends messages that glamorize violence ..." [Kansas City Metro North, Missouri, #20, Native American, 12]
    "television and media body images ..." [Orange County, California, #15, white, 13]
    "media depictions of teenagers ..." [Illinois, #2, Hispanic, 12]
    "pressure from the media ..." [Green Bay, Wisconsin, #66, white, 13]
    "... too perfect." [Green Bay, Wisconsin, #66, white, 13]
    "body images that tell girls to be perfect ..." [Kalispell, Montana, #21, white, 14]
    "perfection (TV images) ..." [Cobb County, Georgia, #7, black, 12]
    "We are also faced with always having to look beautiful ..." [Delaware, #9, white, 15]
    "compare themselves to movie stars ..." [Kalispell, Montana, #9, Native American, 14; suburban Milwaukee, #15, white, 13]

11. "You can pick up any magazine ..." [Carson City, Nevada, #20, no age or race given]
    "between healthy and fit ..." [Massachusetts, #7, Asian American, 15]
    "staying healthy while society tells you to be skinny ..." [West Virginia, #2, white, no age given]

12. "I wish people at my school were open ..." [Willimantic, Connecticut, #10, white, 16]

13. "We women in general are the masters ..." [Western New York, #38, black, 15]

   "We need to fight the battles ..." [Massachusetts, #1, Asian American, 15]

   "to be remembered as fighters ..." [Minneapolis, Minnesota, #38, white, 18]

Chapter Two

....

1. 54 percent of the Hispanic and 45 percent of the African American pregnancy responses are from girls ages 11-13; 30 percent of the white responses and 27 percent of the Asian American pregnancy responses are from girls in this age range.

2. A national study of teen pregnancy conducted by the National Center for Health Statistics in 1998 found that teen birth rates dropped in every state and across all races in the early 1990s, with births to African Americans at the lowest level ever recorded. But those rates vary widely across the country, from 28.6 per 1,000 women in Vermont to 105.5 per 1,000 women in the District of Columbia for teens ages 15 to 19. The decline in the teen birth rate was less dramatic for Hispanic and white girls than for African Americans. Furthermore, as Advocates for Youth describe in their 1999 study tour on teen pregnancy, the United States has a far higher teen pregnancy and abortion rate—eight times that of the Netherlands, for example—other than Western, industrialized nations. They found that teens in more sexually "open" societies actually initiate sex later, at an average age of 17.7 in the Netherlands, as compared to an average age of 15.8 in the United States. See Judy Mann, "Wanted: A Realistic Attitude Toward Sex," *The Washington Post,* 17 January 1999, C-14.

   On the differences between teen parenthood in the suburban, middle-class context and the urban African American community, for example, see Judith Musick, "Adolescent Parenthood and the Transition to Adulthood," in Julia Graber et al., eds., *Transitions Through Adolescence: Interpersonal Domains and Contexts* (Mahwah, New Jersey: Lawrence Erlbaum Associates, 1996): 201-231.

3. 264 respondents (39 percent) of the overall Question 4 sample dispensed some kind of advice about sex or pregnancy. The racial/ethnic breakdown

for those offering their peers advice on these matters is as follows (listed in order of frequency):

115 African American girls (53 percent of the African American sample),

77 Hispanic girls (47 percent of the Hispanic respondents),

17 Native American girls (38 percent of the Native American sample)

44 white girls (23 percent of the white sample), and

11 Asian Americans (21 percent of the Asian American respondents).

4. "there are more important things than boys ..." [Illinois, #17, black, 15]

"sex and boys ..." [Illinois, #17, black, 15]

"You don't need boys in your life ..." [Willimantic, Connecticut, #25, black, 13]

"You don't need a boy to make you feel good ..." [Tampa, Florida, #38, black, 16]

5. Warnings about men's manipulative, predatory behavior may have some basis in the trend toward older men fathering the children of teenage girls. Contrary to the popular image of teen pregnancy as the result of impetuous, reckless encounters or "slips" between peers of the same age, some studies have found a disparity between the father's and the teen mother's age. A 1996 study found that adult men (age 20 or older) fathered two-thirds of the infants born to school-aged mothers in California in 1993. See Mike Males and S.Y. Chew, "The Ages of Fathers in California Adolescent Births, 1993," *American Journal of Public Health* 86, no. 4 (April 1996): 565-568.

"after only one thing ..." [Roswell-Alpharetta, Georgia, #3, Hispanic, 14]

"sneaky" [St. Tammany Parish, Louisiana, #16, black, 12]

"boys won't stay after pregnancy ..." [California, #37, Hispanic, 15]

"boys don't want females for nothing other ..." [Washington, D.C., #8, black, 15]

"Boys don't want love. ... They only want one thing ..." [North Carolina, #11, black, 13]

"The nicer the guy ..." [Nassau/Suffolk Counties, New York, #75, Hispanic, 14]

"All guys are not nice. They may act that way, but ..." [Indianapolis, #11, black, 13]

6. "rush to be grown up" [suburban Milwaukee, #3, black, 11]

"You have your whole life to get pregnant ..." [Nassau/Suffolk Counties, New York, #70, black, 13]

"Wait until you finish high school ..." [Nassau/Suffolk Counties, New York, #70, black, 13]

"Sex does not make you a woman ..." [Cobb County, Georgia, #21, black, 12]

7. "it is hard to have a child ..." [Covina, California, #58, Hispanic, 14]
   "having a child is tough" [Covina, California, #58, Hispanic, 14]
   "If you have a baby ..." [Aurora, Illinois, #22, black, 15]
   "Pregnancy and raising kids is not as easy ..." [Western New York, #35, Hispanic, 14]
   "Teen pregnancy is no joke ..." [Nassau/Suffolk Counties, New York, #31, black, 13]

8. "feels to have a baby" [Aurora, Illinois, #22, black, 15]
   "how it is to be taking care of a baby ..." [Central Brevard County, Florida, #5, black, 16]
   "how it feels to be pregnant" [Aurora, Illinois, #23, Hispanic, 14; Massachusetts, #22, Hispanic, 13]
   "how it feels to have a baby in junior high ..." [Covina, California, #30, Hispanic, 14]
   "Is it hard being a teen mother?" [St. Tammany, Louisiana, #12, black, 12]
   "How can they manage to go to school ..." [Washington, D.C., #10, black, 15]
   "I want to hear about girls who've had kids ..." [Minneapolis, Minnesota, #7, black, 14]
   "How is their life with a baby?" [Tampa, Florida, #10, black, 12]

9. The term "choice" is used here advisedly, since it is quite clear that these respondents are raising "pregnancy" as an issue or struggle and are not endorsing that their peers actually *should* choose early parenthood as an optimal decision. But the idea of "choice" captures the girls' earnest interest in hearing about how other girls made what they describe as decisions and choices about parenthood. It also captures their suspicion that some of their peers are thinking of pregnancy and early parenthood as an attractive, or at least an ambivalent, condition.

10. "Why do some of them *have to have* ..." [Northern Westchester County, New York, #37, black, 16]
    "Why do most girls always ..." [Washington, D.C., #1, black, 13]
    "Why do other girls that have babies ..." [Western New York, #38, black, 15]

"anything, maybe something that would really make me not want to have kids ..." [Willimantic, Connecticut, #41, Hispanic, 13]

11. "Why do girls need to have a baby at a young age ..." [Minneapolis, Minnesota, #53, Hispanic, no age given]
"Why [do] some girls get pregnant ..." [Illinois, #24, Hispanic, 17]
"Some teenage females face neglect ..." [Philadelphia, #17, black, 16]

12. Douglas Kirby, No Easy Answers: Research Findings on Programs to Reduce Teen Pregnancy (Washington, D.C.: National Campaign to Prevent Teen Pregnancy, 1997): 14, reviews teen pregnancy prevention programs in school. Although an "abstinence only" approach is gaining in popularity, Kirby notes that "there does not currently exist any published scientific research demonstrating that [programs using such an approach] have actually delayed (or hastened) the onset of sexual intercourse or reduced any other measure of sexual activity." Conversely, "the overwhelming weight of the evidence demonstrates that programs that focus upon sexuality, including sex and HIV education programs, school-based clinics, and condom availability programs, do not increase any measure of sexual activity." A report by the American Welfare Association similarly found that "only programs that include both abstinence education and information about birth control have been reliably shown to work." See Judith Havemann, "Simply Preaching Abstinence Doesn't Cut Teenage Pregnancy Rate," The Washington Post, 24 March 1997, A-7, for a review.

13. Of the 44 white girls who dispense some sort of advice about sex and pregnancy, 11 urge girls to "wait to have sex," and 27 offer more general information or advice about the "dangers" of sex because of pregnancy, STDs, violence, or AIDS. Of the 11 Asian American respondents who write about sex and pregnancy, 5 urge girls to "wait to have sex" and 4 provide information about risks and dangers associated with sex.

14. "how dangerous it is to have sex ..." [Delaware, #16, white, 13]
"the threats of sex" [Roswell-Alpharetta, Georgia, #12, white, 12]
"dangers in sex and drugs" [Salt Lake City, Utah, #31, white, 15]
"sex is not a game" [Kansas City Metro North, Missouri, #50, white, 16]
"more about the dangers of having sexual relationships" [Nassau/Suffolk Counties, New York, #92, white, 14]
"I've seen a friend of mine get pregnant at age 15 ..." [York County, Pennsylvania, #4, white, 13]

15. "what to do in an uncomfortable situation ..." [Indianapolis, #13, white, 13]
    "when a boy keeps asking you to go out ..." [Salt Lake City, Utah, #4, white, 11]
    "about rape and sex ..." [Nassau/Suffolk Counties, New York, #86, white, 13]
    "how much guys will take advantage of you ..." [Port Huron, Michigan, #3, white, 12]
    "shouldn't go out with boys ..." [California, #32, white, 12]
    "self-defense" [Pocono Area, Pennsylvania, #14, white, 12]
    "how to defend yourself" [St. Tammany, Louisiana #87, white, 12]

16. Researcher Judith Musick, for example, has observed that African American girls growing up in relatively cohesive, if low-income, urban communities may experience a positive pressure to have a child as a way of "belonging" to their community as much as they may lack incentives not to postpone having a child. See Bertram J. Cohler and Judith Musick, "Adolescent Parenthood and the Transition to Adulthood," in Julia A. Graber et al, eds., *Transitions Through Adolescence: Interpersonal Domains and Context* (Mahwah, New Jersey: Lawrence Erlbaum Associates, 1996): 201-233.

17. According to Child Trends, Inc., among young women who gave birth during high school, the majority (62 percent) dropped out at some point. Hispanic teenagers who are pregnant are more likely to drop out (71 percent) than white teens (64 percent) or black teens (54 percent). See Child Trends, Inc., *Facts at a Glance* (Washington, D.C.: Child Trends, Inc., 1996).

18. "There is a lot of pressure on teenage girls to have sex ..." [Aurora, Illinois, #3, white, 14]

19. This report counts in the "sexual harassment" category only those responses that explicitly use the term. Many other girls cite incidents of harassment but do not identify it as such.

20. *Hostile Hallways: The AAUW Survey on Sexual Harassment in America's Schools* (Washington, D.C.: American Association of University Women Educational Foundation, 1993); Leslie R. Wolfe, "Girl Stabs Boy at School: Girls and the Cycle of Violence," *Women's Health Issues* 4, no. 2 (1994): 109-116; Leslie R. Wolfe and J. Tucker, *Victims No More: Girls Fight Back Against Male Violence* (Washington, D.C.: Center for Women Policy Studies, 1997).

21. "In seventh grade, a group of boys made up a 'flat chest club' ..." [Illinois, #22, white, 15]

22. See *Hostile Hallways: The AAUW Survey on Sexual Harassment in America's Schools* (Washington, D.C.: American Association of University Women Educational Foundation, 1993); Valerie E. Lee, et. al., "The Culture of Sexual Harassment in Secondary Schools," *American Education Research Journal* 33, no. 2 (Summer 1996): 383-417.

23. "Stop boys from hurting girls ..." [Toledo, Ohio, #16, black, 14]
    "a school where the adults ..." [Kansas City Metro North, Missouri, #50, white, 16]

24. "teachers and authorities [aware] that this isn't just one big joke ..." [California, #7, white, 16]
    "make teachers REACT when students do/say things ..." [Gilroy, California, #18, white, 15; emphasis in original]
    "pay more attention to the people ..." [Northern Westchester County, New York, #36, Asian American, 12]

25. "I wish there were less sexual disrespect ... I wish we had a specific rule ..." [Illinois, #4, white, 16]
    "that if a girl is sexually harassed ..." [Nassau/Suffolk Counties, New York, #3, Hispanic, 14]
    "stronger laws or laws about put-downs ..." [North Carolina, #39, black, 13]

26. See Nan Stein, *Secrets in Public: Sexual Harassment in Public (and Private) Schools* (Wellesley: Center for Research on Women, 1993); Nan Stein, *Bullyproof: A Teacher's Guide on Teasing and Bullying for Use With Fourth and Fifth Grade Students* (Wellesley: Center for Research on Women, 1996).

27. These answers are too ambiguous to identify the speaker or context, in many cases.

28. "Can I feel on you?" [Cobb County, Georgia, #21, black, 12]
    "Somebody told me they wanted to ..." [Covina, California, #31, Hispanic, 13]
    "when they say, 'Have you ever heard ...'" [Pocono Area, Pennsylvania, #14, white, 12]
    "Do girls like to get their breasts ..." [Nassau/Suffolk Counties, New York, #6, Hispanic, 13; emphasis in original]

29. "don't put out with guys" [Arizona, #18, white, 14]
    "My boyfriend pressured me ..." [Illinois, #39, black, 17]
    "this girl said that I am a slut ..." [Illinois, #29, black, 12]

30. "I was at a sleepover ..." [Auburn, California, #14, white, 14]

31. As researcher Lee Ann Bell notes, African American students may see
    themselves more readily as members of a community within school and
    therefore may be more likely to comment on the overall social, academic,
    and cultural quality of their relations with male peers, especially. See Lee
    Ann Bell, "Changing our Ideas about Ourselves: Group Consciousness-
    Raising With Elementary School Girls as a Means of Empowerment," in
    Christine Sleeter, ed., *Empowerment Through Multicultural Education*
    (Albany, New York: SUNY Press, 1991).

32. "At my school, people can't be just friends ..." [Salt Lake City, Utah, #11,
    white, 11]

33. "males and females com[ing] together ..." [Washington, D.C., #5, black,
    16]
    "let[ting] us communicate more ..." [Willimantic, Connecticut, #23, black,
    12]
    "Men [should] stop thinking they can take over ..." [Detroit, #10, black, 14]
    "the way boys are during lessons ..." [Montana, #14, black, 13]
    "how boys act about sex ..." [Benicia-Vallejo, California, #23, black, 11]

34. "I wish that every girl who enjoys her sexuality ..." [Willimantic,
    Connecticut, #22, white, age not given]

35. "How many girls actually WANT ..." [Salt Lake City, Utah, #23, white, 13;
    emphasis in original]
    "would like to know if other girls feel ..." [St. Tammany Parish, Louisiana,
    #2, white, 14]
    "think having sex is fun?" [Detroit, Michigan, #27, black, 14]
    "why ... girls have sex?" [South Carolina, #17, white, 13; Illinois, #61,
    black, 12]

36. Researcher Lynn Phillips confirms that girls have internalized ideas about
    sexual activity with negative repercussions. See *The Girls Report: What We
    Know and Need to Know About Growing Up Female* (New York: National
    Council for Research on Women, 1998): 48.

37. "educate everyone that there are other ways ..." [Indianapolis, #8, mixed race, 14]

   "kissing in middle school could lead ..." [Detroit, #8, black, 12]

   "sex leads to all types of diseases ..." [Philadelphia, #9, black, 15]

38. "I am confused about what's too far. I *know not to have sex* ..." [Auburn, California, #14, white, 14]

39. See Lynn Phillips, *The Girls Report*; Michelle Fine, "Sexuality, Schooling, and Adolescent Females: The Missing Discourse of Desire," *Harvard Educational Review* 58, no. 1 (1988): 29-53; Michelle Fine, "White Li(v)es: Looking for a Discourse of Male Accountability," in M. Lykes et. al., eds., *Unmasking Social Inequalities: Victims and Resistance* (Philadelphia: Temple University Press, 1994); Pamela Haag, *Consent: Sexual Rights and the Transformation of American Liberalism* (Ithaca: Cornell University Press, 1999). M. Cherland notes in *Private Practices: Girls Reading Fiction and Constructing Identity* (London: Taylor and Francis, 1994): 41, on sexual harassment: "Instead of telling the child what she must do, the culture tells her what she is. MTV, the television news, novels, fashion advertisements, older relatives and the boys at school all told Oak Town girls what they were: powerless people whose bodies were 'naturally' the object of others' desires. It is not surprising, therefore, that most accepted the practice of sexual harassment."

40. "I want to know how to turn down boys nicely ..." [Tampa, Florida, #22, Hispanic, 14]

   "I want to know how to say no ..." [Auburn, California, #25, Asian American, 18]

41. "women's worries about [appearing] nice to men" [California, #7, white, 16]

   "Some girls are being forced into sex ..." [Nassau/Suffolk Counties, New York, #66, black, 13]

   "boys ... can talk you into doing something ..." [Detroit, #14, black, 12]

42. "how to resist evil temptations" [St. Tammany Parish, Louisiana, #1, white, 15]

   "I used to run away a lot ..." [Kansas City Metro North, Missouri, #29, white, 16]

43. "Guys can get too strong ..." [Illinois, #28, white, 12]

   [sexual pressure] "is everywhere ... You have to be the one ..." [Delaware, #9, white, 15]

44. "women always have to worry ..." [California, #7, white, 16]
"I know that it is hard to say 'no' ..." [Covina, California, #15, white, 13]

45. "Once someone told me to have sex ..." [Benicia-Vallejo, California, #13, Hispanic, 13]
"I was dating this boy ..." [Tampa, Florida, #11, black, 13]

46. I get called stuck up a lot ..." [Minneapolis, Minnesota, #14, black, 15]
" ... Even if you're making out with your boyfriend ..." [Kansas City Metro North, Missouri, #35, white, 15]

47. "My friends saw this kid from school ..." [Toledo, Ohio, #7, white, 14]

48. "Some guy I just met told me he loves me ..." [Minneapolis, Minnesota, #8, Hispanic, 14]

49. "teach boys how to act" [Salt Lake City, Utah, #24, Middle Eastern, 14]
"give education for boys treating girls" [Northern Westchester County, New York, #5, Asian American, 12]
"teach boys not to pressure their girlfriends ..." [Salt Lake City, Utah, #7, Hispanic, 14]
"Young men need to learn respect ..." [Philadelphia, #8, white, 16]

50. As Michelle Fine underscores, it is difficult for girls to genuinely "say no" if they have no concept of how they would "say yes"—in other words, if they do not perceive themselves as sexual subjects.

Chapter Three

....

1. Judith Rich Harris, *The Nurture Assumption: Why Children Turn Out the Way They Do* (New York: Free Press, 1998). Harris' study, although it attracted substantial press attention, is based on little research and is mostly anecdotal. However, the dominance of peer influences over adolescents is described more subtly and persuasively in Patricia Hersch, *A Tribe Apart: A Journey Into the Heart of American Adolescence* (New York: Fawcett Books, 1999). Hersch underscores, in contrast to Harris, that adolescents in wealthy suburbs confront many of the same peer pressures and dangers as adolescents in urban or less affluent areas.

2. "lack of guidance from elders" [Massachusetts, #11, white, 13]
   "tons of pressure ..." [Indianapolis, #4, black, 12]
   "not feeling loved enough" [North Carolina, #42, Native American, 13]

3. "I would like girls to know ..." [California, #1, white, 13]
   "that your mom is your best friend ..." [suburban Milwaukee, #2,
      Hispanic, 13]

4. Margaret J. Finders similarly notes in *Just Girls: Hidden Literacies and Life in Junior High* (New York: Teachers College Press, 1997): 39-40, that working-class girls in her qualitative study seemed to maintain deeper ties to family and to their mothers than the generalization about adolescent peer relations would suggest.

5. On migration, obligation, and family experience, see, for example, Nazli Kibria, *Family Tightrope: The Changing Lives of Vietnamese Americans* (Princeton: Princeton University Press, 1993) and *International Migration Review* 28, no. 108 (1994) special issue on "The New Second Generation."

6. The percentage of 41 is lower than the numbers because some girls mentioned more than one of the three categories in their Question 1 answer: They are counted only once in the percentage figure.

7. "if they are popular or not, if ..." [Arizona, #26, white, 12]

8. 29 percent of the African American sample and 39 percent of the Native American populations cite these two issues.

9. Six percent of the Question 5 sample overall "want to know" from other girls how to handle peer pressure. Whites and Asian Americans were over-represented in this response: 9 percent of the white sample and 8 percent of the Asian American respondents give this answer.

10. "pressure to act in a certain way ..." [Massachusetts, #1, Asian American, 15]
    "What I mean by 'clique' is ..." [Green Bay, Wisconsin, #78, Native
       American, 14]

11. "Self-image and how other people see you ..." [Illinois, #88, white, 13]

12. "To be a part of the crowd ..." [Nassau/Suffolk Counties, New York, #66,
       black, 13]

"You are too busy trying to impress ..." [Kansas City Metro North, Missouri, #21, white, 14]

"pressure to have a boyfriend ..." [Massachusetts, #1, white, 15]

13. "being your *own* person while still being accepted ..." [West Virginia, #2, white, no age given]

"deciding when you're going to follow the crowd and when ..." [Arizona, #37, white, 13]

"I would like to know which parts ..." [Auburn, California, #33, white, 17]

"can look through all of the acts and walls you've built ..." [Kansas City Metro North, Missouri, #30, white, 16]

14. "Sometimes your friends can be idiots ..." [Illinois, #71, white, 13]

15. "It's easier to be yourself and not wear ..." [York County, Pennsylvania, #17, white, 14]

"If you act *like yourself* ..." [Illinois, #22, white, 15]

"would like to know from other girls how ..." [Nassau/Suffolk Counties, New York, #69, white, 13; emphasis in original]

16. "being a good person and a good student will get you farther ..." [Huntington, Pennsylvania, #4, white, 14]

"Don't worry about what other people think of you ..." [Illinois, #88, white, 13]

17. "[Don't] let other people's opinions get to you ..." [Indianapolis, #46, white, 13]

"When someone tries to cause a fight ..." [Gilroy, California, #27, white, 14]

"You should remain calm ..." [Northern Westchester County, New York, #49, white, 11]

18. "When something is happening ..." [Northern Westchester County, New York, #48, white, 15]

"There is nothing like lying ..." [Arizona, #31, Hispanic, 12]

"I wish that we could have all the girls get together in a big room ..." [Nassau/Suffolk Counties, New York, #7, white, 13]

"Other girls should know that whatever boys say to you ..." [Nassau/Suffolk Counties, New York, #1, Hispanic, 13]

19. "Ignoring the insults or sexism ..." [Toledo, #15, Middle Eastern, 12]

"At one point in my life ..." [Orange County, California, #13, Middle Eastern, 16]

20. "A senior boy used to yell ..." [Morristown, New Jersey, #4, Asian American, 16]

21. "For the past three years, I've learned ..." [California, #2, Asian American, 16]

22. "People will accept you even if you're different ..." [Kalispell, Montana, #21, white, 14]

23. "Don't give a damn ..." [Salt Lake City, Utah, #10, white, 14]

24. "I would like to know that other girls ..." [West Virginia, #11, white, no age given]

25. "How many feel ..." [Arizona, #19, white, 13]

26. "Are they stressing ..." [Covina, California, #54, Asian American, 13]

27. "Have they ever been ..." [Green Bay, Wisconsin, #5, white, 14]

28. "I would like to know from girls my age ..." [Orange County, California, #19, white, 15]

29. *Shortchanging Girls, Shortchanging America* (Washington, D.C.: American Association of University Women, 1991).

30. "to have high self-esteem ..." [Salt Lake City, Utah, #22, white, 15]

31. "how [girls] present themselves" [Puget Sound , Washington, #15, black, 12] "carry themselves" [Benicia-Vellajo, California, #42, black, 13] "respect themselves and others" [Cobb County, Georgia, #22, black, 13]

32. "If you know that you have respect ..." [Illinois, #60, "mixed," 16] "[Girls] need to respect themselves and others ..." [Illinois, #60, black, 15; Massachusetts, #24, black, 14]

33. Drawing on resiliency theory, researcher Janie V. Ward similarly argues that violence among African American adolescents can be described and combated as a violation of a historical and cultural ethic of care and mutual

support in the African American community. See Janie V. Ward, "Cultivating a Morality of Care in African American Adolescents: A Culture-Based Model of Violence Prevention, *Harvard Educational Review* 65, #2 (Summer 1995): 175-88.

34. "Another person's opinion does not rule over your own ..." [Nassau/Suffolk Counties, New York, #66, black, 13]

35. "need to be shown respect like any adult ..." [South Carolina, #8, black, 14]

36. A 1999 study has found that drug use is slowing down among teens in the United States after dramatic increases in the 1980s. The research, underwritten by the National Institutes of Health, showed a decrease among eighth graders who reported using any illegal drugs over the past year from 23 percent in 1996 to 21 percent in 1998. See "Monitoring the Future," www.isr.umich.edu.

37. There is not a great deal of variation by urban/non-urban or by age on the mention of peer pressure in Question 1. A larger percentage of girls citing peer pressure are 13- and 14-year-olds, but these ages also predominate in the sample overall, so the distribution in effect is proportionate across the age groups.

38. Multiple responses and codes per respondent were noted, so percentages will not total 100.

39. "when females stick together ..." [Philadelphia, #11, black, 15]

40. "the chain of sympathy" [Ann Arbor, Michigan, #39, white, 11]
    ""It's girls who see another friend or even someone they don't know ..." [Arizona, #47, Hispanic, 14]
    "girls helping girls through tough situations ..." [Roswell-Alpharetta, Georgia, #5, white, 14]
    "sisters helping sisters in time of need ..." [Detroit, Michigan, #23, black, 14]

41. "All girls from all cultures ..." [Philadelphia, #30, Hispanic, 13]

42. "You could tell them your problems ..." [Rapid City, South Dakota, #25, Native American, 12]

43. " … to have fun with your girlfriends …" [Huntington, Pennsylvania, #12, white, 12]

44. "someone who is there for you (blood or not) …" [Northern Westchester County, New York, #45, black, 12]
    "being in the position of sister to the community …" [Salt Lake City, Utah, #27, black, 12]
    "sisterly relationship with your girlfriends …" [Nassau/Suffolk Counties, New York, #5, Hispanic, 14]
    "blood-related siblings or extremely close friends" [Montana, #57, Native American, 14]
    "It is someone you can confide in as if they were your real sister" [Kansas City Metro North, Missouri, #55, Asian American, 14].

45. "shared feelings and ideas …" [Massachusetts, #3, white, 15]
    "to love one another and to always have a friend to lean on …" [Kansas City Metro North, Missouri, #36, white, 16]
    "a close 'girlfriend'" [North Carolina, #4, white, 14]
    "It is someone you are close to and you believe in them …" [Rapid City, South Dakota, #16, white, 14]
    "two best friends that are really close …" [Rapid City, South Dakota, #40, Native American, 11]

46. "tell people secrets without having the fear …" [Arizona, #25, white, 11]
    "where you get to know someone so well …"
    "tell people secrets …" [Toledo, Ohio, #7, white, 14]
    "a girlfriend who you can always talk to …" [Huntington, Pennsylvania, #4, white, 14]

47. "respect among each other" [Delaware, #11, black, 13]
    "All the sisters need to stick …" [Benicia-Vellajo, California, #42, black, 13]
    "a pact between women of trust and understanding …" [California, #14, white, 14]

48. "Sisterhood is African American females getting …" [St. Tammany Parish, Louisiana, black, 15]
    "when girls of any age can get together …" [Washington D.C., black, 13]
    "making all colors come together …" [Delaware, #17, black, 14]

49. "group of women joined together for some purpose …" [Indianapolis, #9, black, 11]

"a huge network of women who are not only a powerful force ..."
[Massachusetts, #1, Asian American, 15]

50. "help you fight your battles" [Cobb County, Georgia, #21, black, 12]
"interact[ing] with society ..." [Philadelphia, #28, black, 16]
"to help out when girls or women need it ..." [Nassau/Suffolk Counties,
New York, #3, Hispanic, 14]

51. "when you're alone with your friends ..." [Nassau/Suffolk Counties, New
York, #66, black, 13]
"more ways to try to get out of things ..." [Philadelphia, #24, black, 15]

52. "Don't have cliques ..." [Western New York, #82, white, 13]
"Have peer helpers ..." [Kansas City Metro North, Missouri, #31, white, 12]

53. David Holmstrom, "Students Take on Clique Busting in Junior High,"
Christian Science Monitor, March 24, 1998, www.csmonitor.com.

Chapter Four

....

1. Judy Cohen and Sukey Blanc et al., *Girls in the Middle: Working to Succeed
in School*, researched by Research for Action, Inc. (Washington, D.C.:
American Association of University Women Educational Foundation,
1996).

2. See Margaret Shih, Todd Pitinsky, and Nalini Ambady, "Stereotype
Susceptibility: Identity Salience and Shifts in Quantitative Performance,"
Psychological Science 10, no. 1 (January 1999): 80-84; Claude M. Steele,
"Race and the Schooling of Black Americans," *Atlantic Monthly* (April
1992): 68-78. Claude M. Steele, "Stereotype Threat and the Intellectual
Test Performance of African Americans," *Journal of Personality and Social
Psychology* 69 (1995): 797-811; Mano Singham summarizes Steele's and
other relevant research on race, ethnicity, gender, and performance in "The
Canary in the Mine: The Achievement Gap Between Black and White
Students," *Phi Delta Kappan* (September 1998): 9-15.

3. AAUW coined this term in 1992, using it to describe issues such as body
image, sexuality, and violence that affect girls but are rarely addressed by
the formal school curriculum. The term first appeared in *How Schools*

Shortchange Girls, researched by the Wellesley College Center for Research on Women (Washington, D.C.: American Association of University Women Educational Foundation, 1992; New York: Marlowe and Company, 1995).

4. Maxine Greene, *Releasing the Imagination: Essays on Education, the Arts, and Social Change* (San Franciso: Jossey-Bass, 1995): 9.

5. Girls would tend to emphasize peer relations in Question 2 as well since these issues appear often in question 1.

6. "I would either like to change the people ..." [Massachusetts, #11, white, 13]

7. See Cornelius Riordan, "The Future of Single-Sex Schools," in *Separated by Sex: A Critical Look at Single-Sex Education for Girls,* (Washington, D.C.: AAUW Educational Foundation, 1998): 53-63, for a discussion of "youth culture" in schools vis-à-vis education reform. Henry Giroux, among other education researchers, has emphasized the social, cultural, and political contexts of school as experienced by students. See, for example, Giroux, *Schooling and the Struggle for Public Life* (Minneapolis: University of Minnesota Press, 1988), and *Ideology, Culture, and the Process of Schooling* (Philadelphia: Temple University Press, 1989).

   "so everyone looks and feels the same ..." [Kalispell, Montana, #61, Native American, 16]

8. 21 percent (7) of the Native American respondents, 20 percent of the white sample, and 17 percent of the Asian American respondents gave such answers; Hispanic respondents contributed fewer such answers: The nine that fell into this category accounted for 6 percent of the Hispanic sample.

9. "Our school has a lot of peer pressure ..." [Arizona #6, white, 12]
   "I wish that everyone didn't follow someone else ..." [Ann Arbor, Michigan, #49, white, 13]
   "[Girls should] not worry so much about the way we look ..." [Nassau/Suffolk Counties, New York, #5, Hispanic, 14]
   "I wish I could change [it so] ... that kids accept you ..." [Willimantic, Connecticut, #26, black, 15]
   "[I wish we would] not have a popular group ..." [California #53, white, 17]

10. " ... Make it a more peaceful environment ..." [Orange County, California, #11, Asian American, no age given]
"I wish that girls at my school would not hate ..." [Cobb County, Georgia, #6, black, 16]
"not so judgmental" [Kenosha, Wisconsin, #32, white, 17]
"everyone can get along and then these kinds of things would not happen ..."[North Carolina, #43, Native American, 12]
"no stuck up girls" [Montana, #26, white, 15]

11. *Hostile Hallways:* 15. Nearly one in four (23 percent) of sexually harassed students say that one outcome was not wanting to attend school and 23 percent report not wanting to talk as much in class.
"to stop the violence and for the youth to learn how to respect ..." [Illinois, #6, black, 11]
"girls joining gangs to show they are just as hard ..." [Minneapolis, Minnesota, #53, Hispanic, no age given]

12. Five percent and six percent of the Hispanic and Native American respondents write of dropping out, compared to only 3 percent of the Question 1 sample overall.

13. See U.S. Department of Education, *No More Excuses: The Final Report of the Hispanic Dropout Project* (Washington, D.C.: 1998). Vice President Al Gore announced in January 1998 an ambitious Hispanic dropout prevention plan that includes more than $60 million for teacher training. Due to logistic and demographic complications, it is difficult for the Department of Education to gather data on Indian/Native American educational outcomes. According to a recent Department of Education publication, "American Indian and Alaskan Native students comprise approximately 1 percent of the total student population in the U.S. ... they are rarely represented in sufficient numbers to permit reliable and valid generalizations about their characteristics." [U.S. Department of Education, Office of Educational Research and Improvement, National Center for Education Statistics, "Characteristics of American Indian and Alaska Native Education," Washington, D.C., March 1997.] However, statistics from 1994 do indicate that the American Indian high school completion rate in 1992, at 82 percent, was lower than that of all other groups, including Hispanics, who had an 88 percent completion rate. See U.S. Department of Education, Office of Educational Research and Improvement, National Center for Education Statistics, *The Condition of Education: 1994* (Washington, D.C.: 1995).

14. "Parents put tons of pressure on girls …" [Massachusetts, #11, white, 13]

15. "I wish the teachers would not give out so much homework …" [Pocono Area, Pennsylvania, #9, white, 14]

16. "people would treat girls the same as boys …" [Salt Lake City, Utah, #28, white, 13]
    "I wish that I could change the way teachers …" [Toledo, Ohio, #15, Middle Eastern, 12]
    "gender is also a barrier used to prevent girls …" [Central Brevard County, Florida, #34, black, 14]

17. "My math teacher said that we Mexicans …" [Orange County, California, #3, Hispanic, 16]
    "My driver's education teacher once told the class …" [Orange County, California, #7, Hispanic, 16]

18. "It is very hard to learn anything when you have guys …" [Illinois, #71, white, 13]
    "In most classrooms, girls are the quiet, studious students …" [Massachusetts, #1, Asian American, 15]

19. "school [be] more challenging" [Ann Arbor, Michigan, #2, black, 15].

20. "I just wish they would make learning fun …" [Kansas City Metro North, Missouri, #21, white, 14]
    "Be more alert with students …" [Tampa, Florida, #62, Hispanic, 11]
    "I wish I could change teachers because half of them don't teach us …" [Illinois, #29, black, 12]
    "I wish that the school could be more understanding …" [Delaware, #8, white, 15]

21. "I wish that teachers didn't put you down …" [Washington D.C., #6, black, age not given]

22. In other words, 8 percent of the Hispanic sample mentions counselors compared to only 1.5 percent and 2 percent of the white and African American samples, respectively.

23. "there would actually be someone that we could actually talk to …" [Orange County, California, #22, Hispanic, 16]

24. "I wish the counselors never said ..." [Philadelphia, #46, black, 17]

25. "Teenage girls feel pressure to do well in school ..." [suburban Milwaukee, #20, Asian American, 12]

26. "Boys are better than girls ..." [Kansas City Metro North, Missouri, #10, white, 13]
    "You're just a girl, though ..." [Ann Arbor, Michigan, #1, white, 15]
    "'She can't because she is a girl' ..." [Green Bay, Wisconsin, #44, white, 16]

27. "Someone once told me that I was not smart enough ..." [Nassau/Suffolk Counties, New York, #36, Hispanic, 13]
    "People thought I was retarded." [Massachusetts, #24, black, 14]
    "I wish my stepmother never would have said ..." [Brainerd, Minnesota, #22, white, 13]

28. On the phenomenon of "acting white," see Signithia Fordham, "Black Students' School Success: Coping with the Burden of Acting White," *The Urban Review* 18, no. 3 (1986); Kassie Freedman, "Increasing African Americans' Participation in Higher Education: African American High-School Students' Perspectives," *Journal of Higher Education* 68, no. 5 (September/October 1997): 523-550.

    "acting like a white girl ..." [Aurora, Illinois, #20, black, 17; Wilmington, North Carolina, #9, Native American, 15; Central Brevard County, Florida, #22, black, 13]
    "Someone said that I thought that I was all that ..." [Tampa, Florida, #22, Hispanic, 14]
    "You can't imagine how much I've been criticized ..." [Kansas City Metro North, Missouri, #20, Native American, 12]

29. "over-achievers" [Green Bay, Wisconsin, #33, white, 13]
    "teacher's pets" [Salt Lake City, Utah, #24, white, 14]
    "A lot of people consider me a *bitch*" [York County, Pennsylvania, #2, white, 16]
    "someone said that I was too brainy *and I don't like boys*." [Indianapolis, Indiana, #27, black, 12]

30. "bitchiness" [Indianapolis, Indiana, #27, black 12]
    "called a slut" ..."When I asked him why ..." [Willimantic, Connecticut, #22, white, no age given]

"By my peers I am considered one of the good/smart kids …"
[Massachusetts, #1, Asian American, 15]

31. 10 are from white girls, 8 from Hispanic, 5 from Asian American, and 2 from Native American respondents.

Researcher Karen Arnold notes, similarly, in a study of high school valedictorians, that African American high achievers were more intent and serious about ensuring their economic survival than their white peers. Notes Arnold, "Female African American valedictorians do not fit the pattern" of "contingency planning" in college around the possibility of having a family in the future. Instead, they "carefully ensured they could survive on their own." Karen Arnold, *Lives of Promise: What Becomes of High School Valedictorians* (San Francisco: Jossey-Bass, 1995): 113.

32. "People in school should come to school and learn …" [Illinois, #15, black, 15]
"School is the most important thing [girls] have …" [Tampa, Florida, #59, Hispanic, 12]

33. "that peers would encourage you to be smart …" [Ann Arbor, Michigan, #30, black, 14]

34. "School is where you get an education, not boyfriends …" [Salt Lake City, Utah, #34, Hispanic, 12]
"Girls need to get their education before having sex." [Delaware, #15, black, 13]
"[Girls need to know] not to get pregnant …" [Tampa, Florida, #25, black, 13]
"All girls my age think about is boys …." [Nassau/Suffolk Counties, New York, #36, Hispanic, 13]

35. Research by Child Trends, Inc., finds that girls who said they expected to be successful in school and to complete college were less likely than those without such plans to become teenage mothers. Not only does becoming a teen mother limit achievement, then, but limited expectations of achievement may limit girls' interest in delaying pregnancy and parenthood. See Child Trends, Inc., "Nonmarital School-Age Motherhood: Family, Individual, and Social Characteristics" (Washington, D.C.: Child Trends, Inc., 1999).

36. "if teens want to do something bad enough they will ..." [Mississippi, #18, white, 15]

"the schools don't control kids, no matter how hard they try" [Kansas City Metro North, Missouri, #40, white, 13]

"mostly a fact of life. The school you go to can't control this. ..." [west central Minneapolis, Minnesota, #3, white, 17]

37. "I don't wish I could change anything ..." [Detroit, Michigan, #55, black, 14]

38. "There is a course in our school for girls ..." [Philadelphia #12, Native American, 17]

"My school is very small so these aren't really issues ..." [California, #1, white, 13]

39. *Hostile Hallways:* 15–17.

40. "more personalized and not so militaristic ..." [Illinois, #34, Native American, 15]

"I wish that there could be a program at all schools ..." [Covina, California, #58, Hispanic, 14].

41. "We should be able to pick our favorite teacher ..." [Delaware, #17, black, 14]

"I wish teachers would be more open to those students ..." [Green Bay, Wisconsin, #56, Asian American, 14].

42. "special class throughout the week where girls could go ..."[Kenosha, Wisconsin, #27, black, 15]

43. "[Schools need] more study groups in the classes ..." [Cobb County, Georgia, #21, black, 12]

"we could have a mediation process ..."[Rapid City, South Dakota, #27, white, 16]

"if [peers] can have meetings with a couple of students ..."[Philadelphia, #30, Hispanic, 13]

44. "I wish girls would be recognized as an issue ..." [Minneapolis, Minnesota, #38, white, 18]

"be more aware of what is happening" [Montana, #39, black, 13]

"Don't ignore issues like [sex] that are real ..." [Nassau/Suffolk Counties, New York, #77, Hispanic, 15]

"I wish I could make the schools more understanding ..." [Aurora, Illinois, #10, white, 14]

"the ways that the school walks around problems ..." [Green Bay, Wisconsin, #65, black, 16]

45. "where they told more than just the facts ..." [Mississippi #27, white, 15]

"just learning the cold facts" [Northern Westchester County, New York, #40, white, 13]

"someone at our school to consult with about sex." [Illinois, #39, black, 17]

"sexuality class for kids to express their feelings." [Aurora, Illinois, #20, black, 17]

46. Hispanic teenagers who are pregnant are more likely to drop out (71 percent) than white teens (64 percent) or black teens (54 percent). See Child Trends, Inc., *Facts at a Glance* (Washington, D.C.: Child Trends, Inc., 1996).

Part of mural produced for Brainerd, Minnesota, Girls Summit, October 3, 1998

Selected Bibliography

Arnold, Karen. *Lives of Promise: What Becomes of High School Valedictorians* (San Francisco: Jossey-Bass, 1995).

Bell, Lee Ann. "Changing our Ideas about Ourselves: Group Consciousness Raising with Elementary School Girls as a Means of Empowerment," in Christine Sleeter, ed., *Empowerment Through Multicultural Education* (Albany, New York: SUNY Press, 1991).

Cherland, M. *Private Practices: Girls Reading Fiction and Constructing Identity* (London: Taylor and Francis, 1994): 41.

Child Trends, Inc. Facts at a Glance (Washington, D.C.: Child Trends, Inc., 1996).

Child Trends, Inc. "Nonmarital School-Age Motherhood: Family, Individual, and Social Characteristics" (Washington, D.C.: Child Trends, Inc., 1999).

Cohen, Jody and Sukey Blanc et al. *Girls in the Middle: Working to Succeed in School,* researched by Research for Action, Inc. (Washington, D.C.: American Association of University Women Educational Foundation, 1996).

Cohler, Bertram and Judith Musick. "Adolescent Parenthood and the Transition to Adulthood," in Julia A. Graber, ed., *Transitions Through Adolescence: Interpersonal Domains and Context* (Mahwah, New Jersey: Lawrence Erlbaum Associates, 1996): 201–233.

Finders, Margaret J. *Just Girls: Hidden Literacies and Life in Junior High* (New York: Teachers College Press, 1997): 39–40.

Fine, Michelle. "Sexuality, Schooling, and Adolescent Females: The Missing Discourse of Desire," *Harvard Educational Review* 58 (1) 1988: 29–53.

Fine, Michelle. "White Li(v)es: Looking for a Discourse of Male Accountability," in M. Lykes, et. al., eds, *Unmasking Social Inequalities: Victims and Resistance* (Philadelphia: Temple University Press, 1994).

Fordham, Signithia. "Black Students' School Success: Coping with the Burden of Acting White," *The Urban Review* 18, no. 3 (1986).

Freedman, Kassie. "Increasing African Americans' Participation in Higher Education: African American High-School Students' Perspectives," *Journal of Higher Education* 68, no. 5 (September/October 1997): 523–550.

Giroux, Henry. *Ideology, Culture, and the Process of Schooling* (Philadelphia: Temple University Press, 1989).

Giroux, Henry. *Schooling and the Struggle for Public Life* (Minneapolis: University of Minnesota Press, 1988).

Greene, Maxine. *Releasing the Imagination: Essays on Education, the Arts, and Social Change* (San Franciso: Jossey-Bass, 1995).

Haag, Pamela. *Consent: Sexual Rights and the History of American Liberalism* (Ithaca: Cornell University Press, 1999).

Harris, Judith Rich. *The Nurture Assumption: Why Children Turn Out the Way they Do* (New York: Free Press, 1998).

Havemann, Judith. "Simply Preaching Abstinence Doesn't Cut Teenage Pregnancy Rate," *The Washington Post,* 24 March 1997, p. A7.

Hersch, Patricia. *A Tribe Apart: A Journey into the Heart of American Adolescence* (New York: Fawcett Books, 1998; Ballantine Books, 1999).

Holmstrom, David. "Students Take on Clique Busting in Junior High," *Christian Science Monitor,* March 24, 1998, www.csmonitor.com.

Hostile Hallways: The AAUW Survey on Sexual Harassment in America's Schools (Washington, D.C.: American Association of University Women Educational Foundation, 1993).

How Schools Shortchange Girls, researched by the Wellesley College Center for Research on Women (Washington, D.C.: American Association of University Women Educational Foundation, 1992; New York: Marlowe and Company, 1995).

Kirby, Douglas. *No Easy Answers: Research Findings on Programs to Reduce Teen Pregnancy* (Washington, D.C.: National Campaign to Prevent Teen Pregnancy, 1997).

Lee, Valerie E., et. al., "The Culture of Sexual Harassment in Secondary Schools," *American Education Research Journal* 33, no. 2 (Summer 1996): 383–417.

Males, Mike and S.Y. Chew, "The Ages of Fathers in California Adolescent Births, 1993," *American Journal of Public Health* 86, no. 4 (April 1996): 565–568.

Mann, Judy. "Wanted: A Realistic Attitude Toward Sex," *The Washington Post,* 17 January, 1999: C-14.

Phillips, Lynn. *The Girls Report: What We Know and Need to Know About Growing Up Female* (New York: National Council for Research on Women, 1998).

Riordan, Cornelius. "The Future of Single-Sex Schools," in *Separated by Sex: A Critical Look at Single-Sex Education for Girls* (Washington, D.C.: AAUW Educational Foundation, 1998): 53–63.

Shih, Margaret, Todd Pitinsky, and Nalini Ambady. "Stereotype Susceptibility: Identity Salience and Shifts in Quantitative Performance," *Psychological Science* 10, no. 1 (January 1999): 80–84.

Shortchanging Girls, Shortchanging America (Washington, D.C.: American Association of University Women, 1991).

Singham, Mano. "The Canary in the Mine: The Achievement Gap Between Black and White Students," *Phi Delta Kappan* (September 1998): 9–15.

Steele, Claude M. "Race and the Schooling of Black Americans," *Atlantic Monthly* (April 1992): 68–78.

Steele, Claude M. "Stereotype Threat and the Intellectual Test Performance of African Americans," *Journal of Personality and Social Psychology* 69 (1995): 797–811.

Stein, Nan. *Bullyproof: A Teacher's Guide on Teasing and Bullying for Use with Fourth and Fifth Grade Students* (Wellesley: Center for Research on Women, 1996).

Stein, Nan. *Secrets in Public: Sexual Harassment in Public (and Private) Schools* (Wellesley: Center for Research on Women, 1993).

U.S. Department of Education. Office of Educational Research and Improvement. National Center for Education Statistics. "Characteristics of American Indian and Alaska Native Education" (Washington, D.C.: March 1997).

U.S. Department of Education, *No More Excuses: The Final Report of the Hispanic Dropout Project* (Washington, D.C.: 1998).

Ward, Janie V. "Cultivating a Morality of Care in African American Adolescents: A Culture-Based Model of Violence Prevention, *Harvard Educational Review* 65, no.2 (Summer 1995): 175–88.

Wolfe, Leslie R. "Girl Stabs Boy at School: Girls and the Cycle of Violence," *Women's Health Issues* 4, no. 2 (1994): 109–116.

Wolfe, Leslie R. and J. Tucker. *Victims No More: Girls Fight Back Against Male Violence* (Washington, D.C.: Center for Women Policy Studies, 1997).

*Author, Reviewers,
Board, and Staff*

About the Author

....

Pamela Haag is acting director of research at the AAUW Educational Foundation. She has researched and published extensively on gender and education and on American cultural and women's history. She has a bachelor's degree from Swarthmore College and a doctorate from Yale University.

Selected Advisers and Reviewers

....

Lee Anne Bell, professor of education, State University of New York at New Paltz. Co-editor, *Teaching for Diversity and Social Justice: A Sourcebook* (Routledge: 1997). Author, "Changing Our Ideas About Ourselves: Group Consciousness Raising with Elementary School Girls as a Means to Empowerment" in *Empowerment through Multicultural Education* (SUNY Press, 1990).

Michelle Fine, professor of psychology and social psychology, Personality Program, CUNY/Graduate Center. Author, *Chartering Urban School Reform: Reflections on Public High School in the Midst of Change* (Teachers College Press, 1994). Co-author with L. Weis, *Beyond Silenced Voices: Class, Race and Gender in United States Schools* (SUNY Press, 1993). Her *Framing Dropouts: Notes on the Politics of an Urban High School* (SUNY Press, 1991) received the Distinguished Book Award from the Society for Research on Adolescence.

Barrie Thorne, professor of sociology and women's studies, University of California-Berkeley. Author, *Gender Play: Girls and Boys in School*

(Rutgers University Press, 1993). Co-editor, *Language, Gender, and Society* (Newbury House, 1983).

Janie Ward, associate professor, Department of Education and Human Services, Simmons College. Co-editor, *Mapping the Moral Domain: A Contribution of Women's Thinking to Psychological Theory and Education* (Harvard University Press, 1988).

Board and Staff

• AAUW EQUITY LIBRARY •

NEW!! Voices of a Generation: Teenage Girls on Sex, School, and Self
Compares the comments of roughly 2,100 girls nationwide on peer pressure, sexuality, the media, and school. The girls were 1997 and 1998 participants in AAUW teen forums called Sister-to-Sister Summits. The report explores differences in girls' responses by race, ethnicity, and age, and offers the girls' action proposals to solve common problems.
$13.95 members/ $14.95 nonmembers.

Gaining a Foothold: Women's Transitions Through Work and College
Examines how and why women make changes in their lives through education. The report profiles three groups—women going from high school to college, from high school to work, and from work back to formal education—using both quantitative and qualitative methods. Findings include an analysis of women's educational decisionmaking, aspirations, and barriers. 100 pages/ 1999.
$11.95 members/ $12.95 nonmembers.

Gender Gaps: Where Schools Still Fail Our Children
Measures schools' mixed progress toward gender equity and excellence since the 1992 publication of *How Schools Shortchange Girls*. Report compares student course enrollments, tests, grades, risks, and resiliency by race and class as well as gender. It finds some gains in girls' achievement, some areas where boys—not girls—lag, and some areas, like technology, where needs have not yet been addressed. 150 pages/1998.
$12.95 members/ $13.95 nonmembers.

Gender Gaps Executive Summary
Overview of *Gender Gaps* report with selected findings, tables, bibliography, and recommendations for educators and policymakers. 24 pages/1998.
$6.95 members/$7.95 nonmembers.

Separated By Sex: A Critical Look at Single-Sex Education for Girls
The foremost educational scholars on single-sex education in grades K-12 compare findings on whether girls learn better apart from boys. The report, including a literature review and a summary of a forum convened by the AAUW Educational Foundation, challenges the popular idea that single-sex education is better for girls than coeducation. 99 pages/1998.
$11.95 AAUW members/$12.95 nonmembers.

Gender and Race on the Campus and in the School: Beyond Affirmative Action Symposium Proceedings
A compilation of papers presented at AAUW's June 1997 college/university symposium in Anaheim, California. Symposium topics include: K-12 curricula and student achievement; positive gender and race awareness in elementary and secondary school; campus climate and multiculturalism; higher education student retention and success; and the nexus of race and gender in higher education curricula and classrooms. 1997.
$19.95 AAUW members/$21.95 nonmembers.

Girls in the Middle: Working to Succeed in School
Engaging study of middle school girls and the strategies they use to meet the challenges of adolescence. Report links girls' success to school reforms like team teaching and cooperative learning, especially where these are used to address gender issues. 128 pages/1996.
$12.95 AAUW members /$14.95 nonmembers.

Growing Smart: What's Working for Girls in School Executive Summary and Action Guide
Illustrated summary of academic report identifying themes and approaches that promote girls' achievement and healthy development. Based on review of more than 500 studies and reports. Includes action strategies, program resource list, and firsthand accounts of some program participants. 60 pages/1995.
$10.95 AAUW members/$12.95 nonmembers.

How Schools Shortchange Girls: The AAUW Report
Marlowe paperback edition, 1995. A startling examination of how girls are disadvantaged in America's schools, grades K–12. Includes recommendations for educators and policymakers as well as concrete strategies for change. 240 pages.
$11.95 AAUW members/$12.95 nonmembers.

Hostile Hallways: The AAUW Survey on Sexual Harassment in America's Schools
The first national study of sexual harassment in school, based on the experiences of 1,632 students in grades 8 through 11. Gender and ethnic/racial (African American, Hispanic, and white) data breakdowns included. Commissioned by the AAUW Educational Foundation and conducted by Louis Harris and Associates. 28 pages/1993.
$8.95 AAUW members/$11.95 nonmembers.

SchoolGirls: Young Women, Self-Esteem, and the Confidence Gap
Doubleday, 1994. Riveting book by journalist Peggy Orenstein in association with AAUW shows how girls in two racially and economically diverse California communities suffer the painful plunge in self-esteem documented in *Shortchanging Girls, Shortchanging America*. 384 pages/1994.
$15.00 AAUW members/$15.00 nonmembers.

Shortchanging Girls, Shortchanging America Executive Summary
Summary of the 1991 poll that assesses self-esteem, educational experiences, and career aspirations of girls and boys ages 9-15. Revised edition reviews poll's impact, offers action strategies, and highlights survey results with charts and graphs. 20 pages/1994.
$8.95 AAUW members/$11.95 nonmembers.